M000094722

Invitation to Languages

Foreign Language Exploratory Program

Conrad J. Schmitt

 Glencoe

New York, New York   Columbus, Ohio   Chicago, Illinois   Peoria, Illinois   Woodland Hills, California

Acknowledgements

The author wishes to express his appreciation to those individuals who reviewed the Japanese chapter of the textbook:

Mikako Kohno, Elkhart Community Schools, Elkhart, IN
Cindy Zyniewicz, Elkhart Community Schools, Elkhart, IN

The editor would like to thank the following individuals for their assistance in the development of this program:

Louis Carrillo
Andrea M. Fuchs, Ph.D.
Patricia Ménard
Mary Root Taucher

Glencoe

The *McGraw-Hill* Companies

Copyright © 2004 by The McGraw-Hill Companies, Inc. All rights reserved. Except as permitted under the United States Copyright Act, no part of this publication may be reproduced or distributed in any form or by any means, or stored in a database or retrieval system, without prior permission of the publisher.

Send all inquiries to:
Glencoe/McGraw-Hill
8787 Orion Place
Columbus, OH 43240-4027

ISBN: 0-07-860578-4 *(Student Edition)*
ISBN: 0-07-860579-2 *(Teacher Edition)*

Printed in the United States of America.

1 2 3 4 5 6 7 8 9 10 027 09 08 07 06 05 04 03

Invitation to Languages

Introduction to Languages 1

Welcome to Spanish! 28

Welcome to French! 94

Welcome to Italian! 164

Welcome to Latin! 204

Welcome to German! 228

Welcome to Japanese! 264

Introduction

1

¡Hola! ¿Qué tal?

Communication

"Hi there! How are ya?" This is a greeting we probably use a hundred times a day to start a conversation with someone. Just think what life would be like if we couldn't speak to each other. We wouldn't be able to if we didn't have a language. Try to imagine life without language or speech. It certainly would be dull! On the other hand, think how much fun it would be to speak more than one language. It would be great to be able to speak to people from other parts of the world. We can if we study another language.

Learning another language is not difficult. It's actually fun. There are many languages we can choose to study because there are many different languages spoken in the world. Everyone has a language. But, just what is language?

Guten Tag. Wie geht's?

Konnichi wa.

Salut! Ça va?

Ciao. Come va?

What is Language?

Spoken Language

In its broadest sense, language is the exchange or transfer of meaning. It is a tool of communication. Spoken language or human speech is produced by the human speech organs and received by the ears. Each day we spend hours speaking and listening to friends, relatives, or strangers. Why do we spend so much time talking and listening to each other? We converse to exchange information, to communicate, and to interact. Language lets us exchange ideas, facts, and even emotions. It is a source of knowledge and a source of enjoyment. Language is one of the most fascinating and essential tools possessed by humans. It is our ability to use language that separates us from the rest of the animal world.

Written Language

Spoken language is the most frequently used method of communication. In addition to speaking and listening, however, we obtain much information and enjoyment from reading. To read, we must rely upon written language. Written language uses symbols to represent spoken language. Spoken language, however, existed for thousands, or perhaps millions of years, before the development of written language.

Writing Systems

Pictographs and Ideographs

The writing system for some languages such as ancient Egyptian, as well as modern Chinese, make use of pictographs and ideographs. A pictograph is a symbol or drawing that represents a specific object such as a fish or a chair. In ancient Egypt, the written word for "sun" was a drawing of the sun. It was impossible, however, to draw pictures to represent all words. For this reason,

pictograph
for fish

rè = sun

yuè = moon

míng = bright

ideographs were developed. An ideograph is a symbol for "non-picturable" things. An ideograph is used to show actions and to convey ideas. For example, the Chinese put together their pictographs for the "sun" and "moon" to form the ideograph that symbolizes "bright."

Alphabets

Other languages, such as English, use the letters of an alphabet for their written language. The Phoenicians and Hebrews were the first to use an alphabet. An alphabet is a series of symbols. The Phoenicians and Hebrews made up a symbol for each syllable of a word. It is from these people that we have the beginning of a true phonetic alphabet. A phonetic alphabet is one in which each letter represents a sound in the spoken language. Let's take a look at some alphabets:

א ב ג ד ה ו ז ח
ט י ך כ ל ם מ
ן נ ס ע ף פ צ
ץ ק ר ש ת ת

Hebrew alphabet

ABCDEFGHIJKLMNOPQRSTUVWXYZ
Roman alphabet

ΑΒΓΔΕΖΗΘΙΚΛΜΝΞΟΠΡΣΤΥΦΧΨΩ
Greek alphabet

АБВГДЕЁЖЗИЙКЛМНОПРСТУФХЦЧШЩЪЫЭЮЯ
Cyrillic alphabet

ا ب ت ث ج ح خ د ذ ر ز س ش ص ض ط ظ ع غ ف ق ك ل م ن ه و ي
Arabic alphabet

Here are some words in each of the above alphabets:

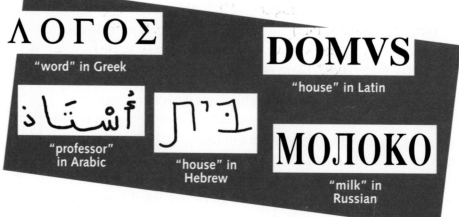

ΛΟΓΟΣ
"word" in Greek

DOMVS
"house" in Latin

أُسْتَاذ
"professor" in Arabic

בַּיִת
"house" in Hebrew

МОЛОКО
"milk" in Russian

4 • *Introduction*

Unlike English, Hebrew and Arabic are read from right to left.

Other Methods of Communication

There are other forms of communication that are neither spoken nor written. Many things that do not involve spoken or written language can convey meaning. For example, a person driving a car stops at a red light. Why does the driver stop? The red light has meaning—it means "stop." On the other hand, a green light indicates "go" and the driver does not stop. The color red stands for "stop" or "danger." The color green stands for "safety" or "go." A transfer of meaning takes place when we see these colors.

Gestures

You are having a conversation with someone. The person you are talking to says nothing, but he uses a gesture. He points his thumb downward. Without a word being said, there is a transfer of meaning. His gesture indicates that he does not agree with you. In a similar conversation, another friend gestures with her thumb up. Without saying a word, she indicates to you that she agrees with what you are saying. She lets you know that you have a good idea.

Sounds

Some non-linguistic forms of communication come close to spoken language. The grunting sound "uh, uh" is an example. It has several meanings depending upon the intonation. Intonation is the melody or pitch that we give to our speech. Have some fun. Say "uh, uh" to convey "yes." Then say the same sound to convey "no." Now, say "uh, uh" with an intonation to convey "maybe."

Symbols

Other non-linguistic forms of communication resemble written language. The dollar sign is an example. When we see "$10," we automatically say "ten dollars." What do the following symbols mean?

Activities

A Work with a classmate. Say a few words to him or her in English. Then ask what message he or she got from what you said. Was it correct? Did a transfer of meaning take place? Did you communicate with each other?

B Let's use some gestures to convey meaning. To the ancient Greeks, a downward nod of the head meant "yes." What do we do to convey "yes"? To the ancient Greeks, an upward nod of the head meant "no." What do we do to convey "no"?

C Use gestures to convey the following meanings.

1. Cool! Right on!
2. You shouldn't do that!
3. Shame!
4. Good-bye.
5. That's it! Enough!
6. Something smells.

D Make a noise or a sound that is not a word to give the following meanings.

1. Yes.
2. No.
3. That's awful!
4. Be quiet.
5. That's not such a good idea.
6. That tastes good.

E Give the meaning of the following symbols.

1.

3.

5.

7.

2.

4.

6.

F Be creative! Draw some pictographs. See if your classmates can guess what words your pictographs represent. If your pictographs are clear, they should be able to guess at the words.

G Make up ideographs to show the following actions or ideas.

1. to throw
2. to sit
3. to love
4. angry
5. happy
6. interesting

H Convert the following math equation into spoken language. Read it aloud.

$$6 \times 2 = 12 \div 3 = 4 + 4 = 8 - 2 = 6$$

I Have some fun and invent your own language.

1. Make up five sounds. Give each of your sounds a meaning. Then share your sounds with classmates. Say your sounds aloud and tell your classmates what they mean.

2. Invent a symbol for each of your sounds. You can use pictographs, ideographs, or letters from your own alphabet. Read each of your symbols by producing the sound it represents.

2

Languages of the World

Every person in the world has a language—a tongue. ^Mother In every city, town, or village of the world people are always talking to one another. They very often express the same ideas, but they all use their own language. People from Nairobi can convey the same message as people from London or Tokyo.

London, England

But in Nairobi, the message is conveyed in Swahili; in London, it's in English; and in Tokyo, it's in Japanese.

Nairobi, Kenya

Each person will use different sounds and words because each language has its own sound system and its own vocabulary. People who share the same language have a great deal in common. Language brings people together.

History of Language

Linguists are scientists who study the many aspects of language. All linguists agree that the origin of human speech is still a mystery. No one knows when or how humans began to speak. No one knows how language started. There are, however, many theories about the origin of language. Some are religious—language was considered a gift from the gods. Others are scientific—language started as an imitation of sounds occurring in nature. For example, humans heard a dog barking. They imitated the sound they heard and said "bow-wow."

Although linguists have not been able to solve the mystery of the origin of language, they have been able to study and analyze almost all of the world's languages.

Language Families

Almost all of the languages of the world can be assigned to families or groups. Languages are assigned to the same family based upon a definite resemblance to each other.

The Indo-European Family

Indo-European is the name given to the family to which English belongs. The Indo-European family consists of languages now spoken in the Americas, most of Europe, and as far eastward as northern India and some parts of Asia. Almost one-half of the world's population speaks a language that belongs to the Indo-European family.

It is thought that in prehistoric times, long before the introduction of written language, speakers of the original Indo-European language formed a closely knit group. They probably lived in what is now known as central Russia. Because of famine, natural disasters, or wars, there were waves of migration. Some people left their homeland and some people stayed. Those who left did not all go in the same direction. They separated into various groups and went different ways. They, therefore, lost contact with one another and their speech began to change. Over the centuries the changes became so great that the original parent language evolved into many new and different languages.

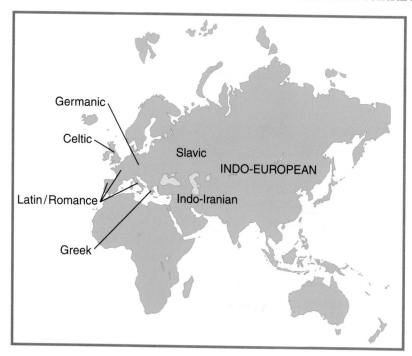

The modern language which is believed to be the closest to the original Indo-European language is Lithuanian. It is spoken in Lithuania, a small and largely rural country on the Baltic Sea.

In most of the Indo-European languages, there is a striking resemblance in the numerals one to ten. The words for close family relationships are also very similar:

English	seven	brother
German	**sieben**	**Bruder**
Latin	**septem**	**frater**
Russian	**CEMb**	**БРАТ**
Sanskrit	**sapta**	**brata**

Within the Indo-European family, there are sub-groups. Examples of some of the larger sub-groups are:

Germanic	Romance	Slavic
German	Latin	Russian
Dutch	Italian	Ukranian
Swedish	Spanish	Polish
Danish	Portuguese	Czech
Norwegian	French	Slovak
Icelandic	Rumanian	Serbo-Croatian
English		Bulgarian

Close Relatives

Some languages are very similar to one another. For example, an Italian speaker and a Spanish speaker could have a conversation together. Each person could speak his or her language and they would be able to understand one another with just a little difficulty. The same would be true for a Portuguese speaker and a Spanish speaker. However, a Spanish, Italian, or Portuguese speaker would not understand a person speaking French or Rumanian. They would have to study French or Rumanian to understand without difficulty.

A Russian, Pole, and Czech could all have a conversation together. Each one could use his or her own language and achieve a fair degree of understanding without great difficulty. The Slavic tongues are more like each other than the languages of most of the other Indo-European sub-groups.

English

English belongs to the western branch of the Germanic group of the Indo-European family. Anglo-Saxon, an old Teutonic or German language, forms the backbone of English. In 1066, however, a very important event took place. This event brought about many changes in the English language. The Normans invaded England from France bringing their language with them. Because of this Norman invasion and conquest, many French and Latin words and grammatical forms came into the English language.

Other Language Families

Another important language family is the Semito-Hamitic family of North Africa and the Middle East. The two most widespread of the modern Semitic languages are Arabic and Hebrew.

The Ural-Altaic family of languages includes Finnish, Estonian, Hungarian, Turkish, and Mongol. The Sino-Tibetan languages of southeastern Asia are Chinese, Thai, Burmese, and Tibetan. Japanese and Korean, the Dravidian tongues of southern India, and the Polynesian languages of the Pacific are all classified separately.

There are three great language divisions in black Africa. They are the Sudanese-Guinean, Bantu, and Hottentot-Bushman. These three families are further subdivided into 800 tribal languages!

The two most widely-used African languages are Hausa of Nigeria and Swahili of the east coast. There is a possibility that one of these two languages will become the common language for all of Africa's black population. It appears that Swahili is already attaining this status. Hindustani has assumed a similar role on the Indian sub-continent where many languages are also spoken.

Swahili sign: "Stop Main Road Turn Left"

Activities

A Explain why it is possible to group many of the world's languages into families.

B It is said that some languages are like first cousins. Others are more like distant cousins. Explain why.

C Does anyone in your family speak a language other than English? If so, find out some information about this language and share it with your classmates. If you can also speak the language, teach a few words and expressions to your classmates.

3

Words

Do you think that you could say something if you didn't know any words? Of course, the answer is "no." Without words, we can't speak. Words are an extremely important part of language. The more words we know, the more feelings and ideas we can express. As you study another language, be sure to learn your vocabulary. If you have the words you need, you'll be able to communicate.

Every language provides words for anything its speakers want or need to say. It will be fun for you to learn them. Some words in other languages are similar to English words and others are very different.

BOOK

das Buch (German)   **liber** (Latin)

el libro (Spanish)   本 **hon** (Japanese)

书 **shū** (Chinese)

kitabu (Swahili)

il libro (Italian)

What is a Word?

A word is one of the most important parts or components of language. A word is defined as the most elementary unit of meaning. It is the simplest thing or element of a language that conveys meaning. A word can be divided into syllables. However, if you hear a syllable by itself, you will get no meaning. For example, *na* is a syllable. Alone it doesn't mean anything. When we hear several syllables together in a word, we do get meaning— "nana." We get meaning, too, when we hear the word "banana."

Rich Languages

A language is considered a rich language if it has an extensive vocabulary—if it has many words. English, for example, is considered to be a rich language. It is estimated that there are about 500,000 words in the English language! Of course, no one knows or uses all of the words. Estimates vary greatly as to the number of words the average person uses on a daily basis. A recent study estimates that the average person uses about 1,200 words. Many linguists, however, have questioned this figure. Some estimates run as high as 35,000 to 70,000 words! The tremendous difference may be due to the confusion between the number of words a person uses (use vocabulary) and the number of words a person recognizes (recognition vocabulary). For every word we use constantly in everyday speech, there are perhaps ten words that we're able to recognize when we hear them or see them in print.

Rich languages have a large number of words to express almost the same concept. In English, we can say beautiful, comely, exquisite, good-looking, gorgeous, handsome, nice, or pretty. How many of these words do you use frequently? Are there others that you can recognize, but don't often use?

Making Words

It is amazing how languages are able to borrow, adapt, and create new words. The German language makes new words by putting several words together. Let's look at some of them:

German	English
Geburt	birth
Tag	day
Geburtstag	birthday
Geschenk	present
Geburtstagsgeschenk	birthday present
Stadt	town, city
haupt	principal
Hauptstadt	capital (principal city)

All words in the Chinese language have only one syllable. They are monosyllabic. The Chinese put many monosyllabic words together to form new words. Some of the combinations are very interesting and philosophical:

Chinese		English
有	yǒu	to have
意思	yìsz	idea
有意思	yǒuyìsz	(have an idea) interesting
没	méi	a part of speech that indicates "not"
没有意思	méiyǒuyìsz	(not have an idea) boring

Coining New Words

The vocabulary or lexicon of a language constantly changes. For example, as technology advances, the vocabulary must change to enable people to describe and work with the new technology. New words have to be coined to express new ideas and things. Recent additions to the English language are:

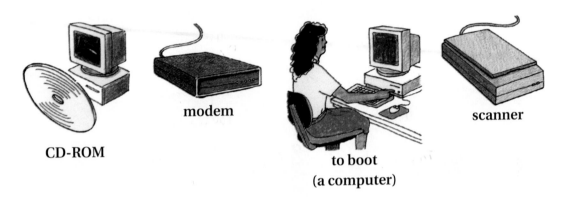

CD-ROM

modem

to boot
(a computer)

scanner

Sometimes two or more words already in use are put together to express a new idea:

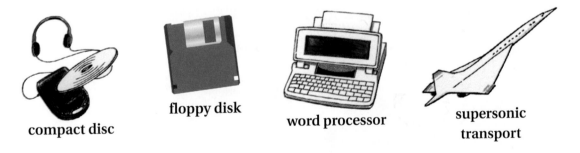

compact disc

floppy disk

word processor

supersonic
transport

Just as new words are invented, other words are often dropped when they identify something that has become obsolete or is no longer used. The expression "to crank a car" is no longer used because cars today are started by turning a key in the ignition.

Borrowing Words

All languages borrow words from each other. Here are some words that have come into English from other languages:

Spanish	*Italian*	*French*	*German*	*Russian*
adobe	prima donna	à la carte	dachshund	babushka
rodeo	stucco	resume	kindergarten	tundra

pizza

tacos

delicatessen

borscht

Many languages also borrow words from English. As you study other languages, you will notice how many English words you will come across.

Spanish	French	Japanese
el béisbol	le sweat-shirt	asuparagasu
el sándwich	le taxi	fasshon
el tenis	le ticket	konpuutaa
el ticket	le week-end	supu

Activities

A Talk to your grandparents or to an older person. Ask them if they use some words today that did not exist when they were children. Make a list of words they give you. Share your list with classmates. Do your lists contain some of the same words? Why?

B The following are words and expressions that were once in common use in English. Do you know what they mean? Explain why these words are no longer used in everyday speech.

1. horse and buggy
2. water wheel
3. well
4. blacksmith
5. outhouse
6. to stoke the stove
7. to crank the shaft

C Ecology is a new science. It describes all living creatures and their relationships with the environment. What are some ecological words that are new to the English language?

D Make a list of words that you think have come from another language. Tell what language.

4

The Structure of Language

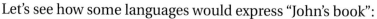

Look at the following phrases in English:

John's book   Mary's pen

In English the 's construction is used to indicate possession. "John's book" means that the book belongs to John. "Mary's pen" means that the pen belongs to Mary, it's Mary's. The 's construction to express possession or ownership is an example of English structure. All languages can express possession, but they do it in a different way. When speaking English, you could say María's pen, Pierre's book, or Hanada-san's pencil. When speaking Spanish, French, or Japanese, however, you cannot say María's, Pierre's, or Hanada-san's. You would not be understood because the 's construction does not exist in these languages.

Let's see how some languages would express "John's book":

English	John*'s* book
French	le livre *de* Jean
Spanish	el libro *de* Juan
German	das Buch *von* Johann
Japanese	Hanada-san *no* hon
Italian	il libro *di* Giovanni
Latin	liber Ioann*i*

Can you tell what languages the books on this page are written in?

What is Structure?

Structure is another important part or component of language. The structure of a language, sometimes referred to as grammar or syntax, is the way in which words are put together to form phrases or sentences. Each language has its own distinctive structure. Structure can vary greatly from one language to another. This is particularly true among languages that do not belong to the same family.

Inflection

Some languages are inflected languages, particularly the ancient tongues. An inflected language makes use of endings attached to words. Latin, for example, is a highly inflected language. Word order is not important in an inflected language. The ending indicates the function of the word in the sentence. In Latin, you could say:

Petrus videt Paulum.

Petrus Paulum videt.

Videt Petrus Paulum.

Regardless of the word order, we know the sentence always means "Peter sees Paul" because the -*us* ending indicates the doer of the action (subject). The -*um* ending indicates the receiver of the action (direct object).

English is not an inflected language, so word order is very important. The word order can change the meaning of the sentence completely:

Peter sees Paul.

Paul sees Peter.

In English, the following word order must be followed:

doer (subject)	action (verb)	receiver (direct object)
Peter	sees	Paul.

In the case of action words or verbs, inflected languages use endings to indicate who does the action and when the action takes place. Let's look at a Latin verb: *cantābimus.* The one word *cantābimus* actually contains three messages. What are they?

1	2	3
cantā (sing)	**bi** (will)	**mus** (we)

Cantā conveys the meaning of the action word—sing; *bi* indicates when the action takes place, in the future—will; *mus* indicates who will perform the action—we.

Modern English drops the endings and isolates the three meanings into three different words:

3	2	1
We	will	sing.

Structural Changes

Languages change because people want to simplify them to make them easier. Languages spoken by many people change more rapidly and drastically than languages spoken by only a few people.

Many languages have dropped endings that existed earlier. Why? When people speak rapidly they tend to drop or eliminate some sounds. When people stopped pronouncing word endings clearly, it became difficult to hear them. If an ending could not be heard in an inflected language, people could not determine the doer and receiver of the action. The meaning of the sentence became unclear. As endings were eliminated, word order became more important. In languages that have very few endings, such as English, word order is crucial.

The Romance languages have kept verb endings, but have dropped the endings for the doer and receiver of the action. However, Russian retains endings in both cases as does German, but in a somewhat different way.

Word Order

Word order in sentences can vary from one language to another. For example, German word order is different from English word order. It is said that German speakers interrupt each other less frequently than do English speakers. The reason for this unproven claim is word order. Key words that convey the important aspects of meaning come at the end of a German sentence. It is difficult to agree or disagree until the listener has heard the entire sentence!

English

I think that you should do your work now.

German

Ich glaube, dass du jetzt deine Arbeit machen sollst.

(I think that you now your work do should.)

Particles

The Japanese language uses many particles. A particle is a small word that indicates how a word functions in a sentence. The particle *no* indicates possession just as the *'s* denotes possession in English:

Hanada-san *no* denwa bangoo   Mr. Hanada's telephone number

The particle *ka* at the end of a Japanese sentence indicates a question:

Hanada-san desu *ka*[?]   Are you Mr. Hanada?

The Chinese language also uses particles. The particle *ma* indicates a question. The particle *bu* attached to a word means "not."

Nǐ lèi ma[?]	Are you tired?
Wǒ búlèi.	No, I'm not tired.
Wǒ bùhěn lèi.	I'm not very tired.

Stress

Stress is the emphasis or force that we give to a sound or a word. In English, more than in most other languages, the stress put on a word in a sentence can change the meaning of the sentence. Read the following sentences aloud. Put the stress on the word indicated in bold. See how the meaning changes.

Sentence	*Meaning*
He would leave now.	He would certainly leave. Maybe you or the others wouldn't but he would.
He would **leave** now.	He would leave rather than do something else.
He **would** leave now.	I know he would leave even though you may think he wouldn't.
He would leave **now.**	He would leave now rather than later.

Tone

The language spoken by the greatest number of people in the world is Chinese. Chinese relies on word order in a sentence since it does not have inflected endings. It does, however, have tones which are extremely important. In the Beijing dialect, each word has four tones. Some are rising tones and others are falling tones. Each tone changes the meaning of the word. Depending upon the tone, the Chinese word *ma* can have the following meanings: mother, horse, flax, or scold. *Ma* can also be added to the end of a statement to turn it into a question.

Beijing, China

Activities

A Look at these Italian and Spanish action words or verbs.
Do you think they retain the types of endings they inherited
from Latin?

Italian
parli   →   parlo
parlavi   →   parlavo

Spanish
hablas   →   hablo
hablabas   →   hablaba

B Look at the verbs to drink, to sing, and to swim in German.
Do they remind you of English in any way? Why?

Ich trinke Wasser.
Ich trank Wasser.
Ich habe Wasser getrunken.

Ich singe mit Hans.
Ich sang mit Hans.
Ich habe mit Hans gesungen.

Ich schwimme im Sommer.
Ich schwamm im Sommer.
Ich bin im Sommer geschwommen.

C As you now know, English has eliminated most endings. There are, however, some words that still change according to their function in a sentence. Choose the correct form in each of the following sentences.

1. That's between you and _____. (her, she)
2. That's between you and _____. (him, he)
3. That's between you and _____. (I, me)
4. _____ and _____ are good friends. (He and I, Him and me)
5. They told _____ the same story. (she and I, her and me)
6. _____ is it? (Who, Whom)
7. _____ did you see? (Who, Whom)
8. He _____ you. (see, sees)
9. You _____ him. (see, sees)
10. They _____ good. (looks, look)

D Read the following sentences aloud putting the stress on the indicated word. Then complete the sentences below.

1. **Mary** hit the ball.
2. Mary **hit** the ball.
3. Mary hit the **ball.**

1. Mary hit the ball. _____ didn't.
2. Mary hit the ball. She didn't _____ the ball.
3. Mary hit the ball, not _____.

E Have some fun. Convert English into an inflected language. Make up a doer ending and a receiver ending. Make up a verb or action ending. Put these endings on English words. Use them to make up your own sentences.

F Read the following short passages. Identify the language.

1. Hwaet! we Gar-dena in geardagem,

   peodcynga brym gefrunon,

   hu pa aepelingas ellen fremedon!

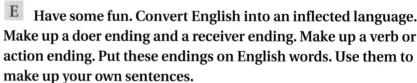

2. Whan that Aprille with his shoures soote

   The droghte of Marche hath perced to the roote,

   And bathed every veyne is swich licour,

   of which vertu engendered is the flour;

The above passages are both in English! The first selection is Old English written down between 500 and 1100 A.D. It is the first three lines of the epic poem *Beowulf*. The second selection is the first four lines of Geoffrey Chaucer's *Canterbury Tales* written in the late 13th century. It is written in Middle English.

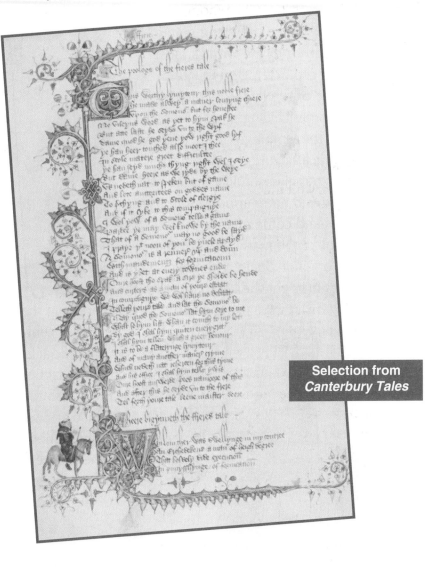

Selection from
Canterbury Tales

Welcome to *Spanish!*

Spanish is the language of more than 350 million people from all over the world. Spanish is sometimes fondly called the "language of Cervantes," the author of the world's most famous novel and character, Don Quijote.

Spanish is one of the five Romance languages. All the Romance languages originally came from Latin, the language of the ancient Romans. Spanish is a beautiful and rich language. It is an extremely useful language and is becoming more and more important in the world of business and commerce.

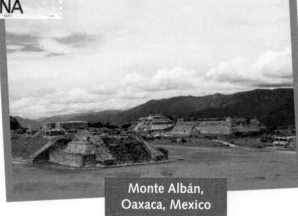

Spanish is spoken in many parts of the world. It had its origin in Spain. The Spanish *conquistadores* and *exploradores* brought the language with them as they explored the Americas in the fifteenth and sixteenth centuries.

Spanish is the official language of most of the countries of Central and South America. It is also the official language of Mexico and several of the larger islands in the Caribbean. Spanish is also the mother tongue of some 37 million people in the United States.

Caracas, Venezuela

PROTEGE LA FAUNA
CORREOS
ESPAÑA

Monte Albán,
Oaxaca, Mexico

Ávila, Spain

Spanish to English

You probably already know many Spanish words. If someone said *hola*, *amigo*, or *adiós*, you would know what they mean, *¿no?* Here are some words that have come into English from Spanish:

adobe	llama	rancho
alpaca	mesa	rodeo
canyon	plaza	sombrero
corral	poncho	

La Paz, Bolivia

1 $Saludos$

Greeting People

—¡Hola!
  —¡Hola! ¿Qué tal?
—Bien, gracias. ¿Y tú?
  —Muy bien.

In Spanish-speaking countries, young people usually shake hands when they meet. Pretend that you are in Spain and shake hands with your classmates.

Actividades

A Get up from your desk and walk around the classroom. Say *hola* to each classmate you meet.

B Work in groups of two. Make up a conversation in Spanish. Greet each other and find out how things are going.

Some greetings are more formal than *hola*. When you greet someone, particularly an older person, you can say:

Buenos días, señora. (A.M.)

Buenas tardes, señorita. (P.M.)

Buenas noches, señor. (late P.M.)

When speaking Spanish, the titles *señor, señora,* and *señorita* are most often used without the first or last name of the person:

Buenos días, señor.

Buenas tardes, señora.

Actividades

A Draw five stick figures. Give each one a name. They will represent your friends, family, and teachers. Greet each of your stick figures properly in Spanish.

B Look at these two photographs of Spanish-speaking people greeting each other. Do they do some of the things we do when they greet one another? Do they do some things that are different? Explain.

Cultura

Spanish Speakers in the U.S.

There are presently more than 37 million people of Hispanic or Latino origin in the United States. The largest number of Hispanics or Latinos are of Mexican birth or ancestry (12,110,000). Puerto Ricans make up the second largest Hispanic group (2,471,000). Spaniards, Dominicans, Central and South Americans together make up the third group (2,200,000). Cuban Americans number more than one million.

A Mexican American family

Puerto Rican Day parade, New York

Cuban Americans

2 ◆ A*diós*

Saying "Good-bye"

—Adiós, José.
—Adiós, Maripaz.

—¡Chao, Juanita!
—Chao. ¡Hasta luego!

The usual expression to use when saying "good-bye" to someone is:

¡Adiós!

If you plan to see the person again soon, you can say:

¡Hasta pronto!　　**¡Hasta luego!**　　**¡Hasta la vista!**

If you plan to see the person the next day, you can say:

¡Hasta mañana!

An informal expression that you frequently hear, especially in Spain and Argentina, is:

¡Chao!

Chao is an Italian expression *(ciao)* that is used in several other European languages.

Actividades

A　Go over to a classmate. Say "so long" to him or her and then return to your seat.

B　Work with a friend. Say *chao* to one another and let each other know that you'll be getting together again soon.

C　Say "good-bye" to your teacher in Spanish and then say "good-bye" to a friend. Don't forget to use a different expression with each person!

Conversando más

—¡Hola, José!
　—¡Hola, Teresa! ¿Qué tal?
—Bien. ¿Y tú?
　—Muy bien, gracias.
—Chao, José.
　—Chao, Teresa. ¡Hasta luego!

Actividades

A   Work with a friend. Speak Spanish together. Have fun saying as much as you can to one another!

B   Look at these two photographs of Spanish-speaking people saying "good-bye." Describe what the people are doing.

Cultura

Common First Names

The following are some common names used for boys and girls in Spanish.

Muchachos

Álvaro, Antonio, Alejandro, Daniel, David, Eduardo, Emilio, Enrique, Felipe, Fernando, Francisco, Gerardo, Ignacio, Jaime, José, Juan, Luis, Manuel, Miguel, Pablo, Pedro, Ricardo, Roberto, Tomás, Vicente

Muchachas

Alejandra, Alicia, Ana, Andrea, Beatriz, Catalina, Clara, Débora, Elena, Guadalupe, Isabel, Josefina, Juana, Leonor, Luisa, María, Marta, Patricia, Pilar, Rosa, Teresa

See if you can find some common Spanish first names in this music club ad.

3 En clase

Identifying Classroom Objects

To find out what something is, you ask:

¿Qué es?

una pizarra

una silla

una hoja de papel (un)

un libro

una computadora

una mesa

un cuaderno

una calculadora

un borrador

una tiza

una goma

un bloc

un lápiz

un bolígrafo

una pluma

una silla

una mochila

To ask for something in a polite way, you say:

Una hoja de papel, por favor.

Actividades

A   Ask a classmate for the following items in Spanish.
Don't forget to ask politely!

1.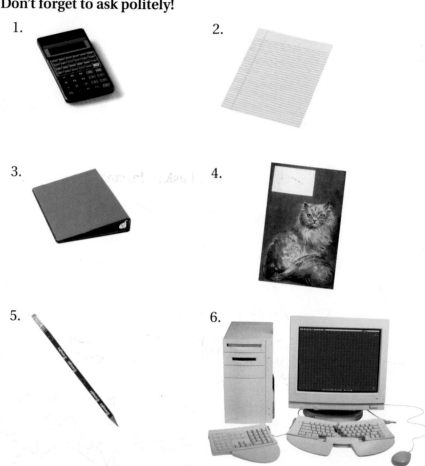

2.

3.

4.

5.

6.

B   Look at each picture and say in Spanish what
each person needs.

Necesita...

1.

2.

3.

$$(x-2)(x^2+2x+4)$$

4.

C   Point to a classroom object and ask a classmate what it is.

Cultura

Schools in Spain and Latin America

In most schools in Spain and Latin America students must wear uniforms. Do you think it's a good rule to have? Do you wear uniforms at your school?

Students outside school, Madrid, Spain

4 Números

Counting in Spanish

0	cero	21	veintiuno	50	cincuenta
1	uno		(veinte y uno)	60	sesenta
2	dos	22	veintidós	70	setenta
3	tres	23	veintitrés	80	ochenta
4	cuatro	24	veinticuatro	90	noventa
5	cinco	25	veinticinco		
6	seis	26	veintiséis	100	cien, ciento
7	siete	27	veintisiete	200	doscientos
8	ocho	28	veintiocho	300	trescientos
9	nueve	29	veintinueve	400	cuatrocientos
10	diez	30	treinta	500	quinientos
				600	seiscientos
11	once	31	treinta y uno	700	setecientos
12	doce	32	treinta y dos	800	ochocientos
13	trece	33	treinta y tres	900	novecientos
14	catorce	34	treinta y cuatro	1.000	mil
15	quince	35	treinta y cinco	2.000	dos mil
16	dieciséis	36	treinta y seis		
	(diez y seis)	37	treinta y siete		
17	diecisiete	38	treinta y ocho		
18	dieciocho	39	treinta y nueve		
19	diecinueve	40	cuarenta		
20	veinte				

Actividades

A   Your teacher will write some numbers on the chalkboard. Then he or she will call out the number in Spanish and ask a student to circle the correct number.

B   Work with a classmate. One of you will count from 30 to 40. The other will count from 70 to 80.

C   Have a contest with a friend. See who can count the fastest from 1 to 100 by tens.

D   Have a contest with a friend. See who can count the fastest from 100 to 1000 by hundreds.

Finding Out the Price

To find out how much something costs, you ask:

—¿Cuánto es la calculadora, señora?

  —Mil doscientos pesos.

—Gracias, señora.

Cultura

Writing Numbers in Spanish

In some parts of the Spanish-speaking world, the use of the period and the comma with numbers is the reverse of that in English.

inglés	español
24.90	24,90
1,000	1.000

See if you can find the numbers written this way in the Spanish rental car ad below.

Ya no hay excusas para quedarse en casa

Con la Tarifa Fin de Semana Flexible podrá alquilar un vehículo en su propia localidad, o al llegar a su punto de destino a través de tren o avión. Ahora con más ventajas que nunca.

España.

 Máxima Flexibilidad; de 2 a 5 días sin límite de kilometraje.

 Podrá disfrutar de su vehículo entre las **12:00 h. del Jueves** y las **12:00 h. del Miércoles.** Debiendo incluir siempre un Sábado o un Domingo en el período de alquiler.

Grupo	Modelo de coche o similar	Número de plazas	Número de puertas	Disponible en Madrid, Barcelona y Málaga	Disponible en Península	Disponible en Baleares	Disponible en Canarias	Asiento niño	Edad mínima 25 años	Radio	Automático	Dirección asistida	Frenos ABS	Airbag	Aire acondicionado	Código C.R.S.	CODIGO TARIFA LF 2 días/por día	LF 3 días/por día	LF 4 días/por día	LF 5 días/por día
A	Opel Corsa Viva 1.2	3	•	•	•											ECMN	5.830	9.750	10.740	12.550
	Fiat Punto 55S	3	•	•	•											ECMN				
	Renault Clio RL 1.2	3	•	•	•											ECMN				
B	Fiat Punto 55S	5	•	•	•			•								EDMN	7.000	10.500	12.890	15.060
	Seat Ibiza CLX 1.4	5	•	•	•			•								EDMN				
	Renault Clio RL 1.2	5	•	•	•			•								EDMN				
C	Fiat Brava 1.4 S	5	•	•	•			•	•							CDMR	8.170	12.250	15.040	17.570
	Renault 19 Driver 1.4	5	•	•	•			•	•							CDMR				
	Seat Córdoba CLX 1.6	5	•	•	•			•	•							CDMR				
D	Opel Astra GLS 1.6	4	•	•	•			•	•							ICMR	9.330	14.000	17.190	20.080
	Lancia Dedra 1.6 LE	4	•	•	•			•	•		•					ICMR				
	Renault 19 S 1.8	4	•	•	•			•	•							ICMR				
E	Renault 19 1.8	4	•	•	•			•	•		•					IDAR	12.670	19.000	23.330	27.250
		4	•	•				•	•							IDAR				
F	Seat Toledo GLX 1.8i	5	•	•				•	•		•					IDMR	12.670	19.000	23.330	27.250
	Seat Toledo SXE 1.8i	5	•	•				•	•		•					IDMR				
G	Opel Vectra GL 1.8 16v	4	•	•	•			•	•		•					SDMR	16.670	25.000	30.700	35.860
	Renault Laguna RT 2.0	5	•	•	•			•	•		•	•	•	•	•	SDMR				
		4	•	•				•	•		•					SDMR				
I	Renault Laguna RXE 2.0	5	•	•	•			•	•	•	•	•	•	•	•	FDAR	17.500	26.250	32.240	37.650
		4	•	•				•	•	•	•	•	•	•	•	FDAR				
EJECUTIVO																PDMR				
J	Opel Omega GL Sedan 2.0	4	•	•	•			•	•	•	•	•	•	•	•	PDMR	18.000	27.000	33.160	38.730
	Renault Safrane RN 2.2 SI	5	•	•	•			•	•	•	•	•	•	•	•	PDMR				
	Renault Safrane 2.2 SI 140 CV	5	•	•	•			•	•	•	•	•	•	•	•	PDMR				
	Lancia K 2.0	4	•	•				•	•	•	•	•	•	•	•					

In Spain and some areas of Latin America, the numbers one and seven are written differently. Look at the photograph below to find these numbers. How are they written?

Actividad

A Work with a classmate. One of you will be the customer and the other will be the clerk at a stationery store. Make up a conversation to buy the following things.

el cuaderno

la calculadora

1200 pesos

40 pesos

la goma

el bolígrafo

3 pesos

9 pesos

7 pesos

el lápiz

900 pesos

la mochila

Cultura

Money Systems

The monetary unit in Spain is the *euro.*

In many Latin American countries the monetary unit is the *peso.* In Venezuela, the monetary unit is named after the famous Latin American hero Simón Bolívar—*el bolívar.*

In Guatemala, the currency is named after the national bird—*el quetzal.*

5 ◆ La cortesía

Speaking Politely

—¡Hola!
   —Dos sodas, por favor.

(The server brings the order.)
—Gracias.
   —No hay de qué.

(*A little later.*)

—¿Cuánto es, por favor?

—Ochenta pesos.

Other ways to express "you're welcome" are:

De nada. **Por nada.**

Actividades

A With a friend, practice reading the three dialogues on pages 45 and 46 aloud.

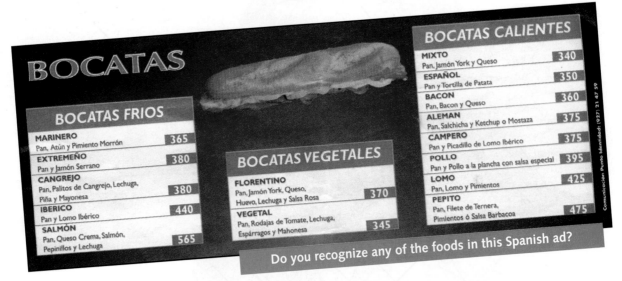

Do you recognize any of the foods in this Spanish ad?

B You are at a café in Playa del Carmen, Mexico. Order the following things. Ask a classmate to be the server.

1. un sándwich

2. un té

3. una soda

4. una limonada

5. una ensalada

C You would like to order the following foods at a Mexican restaurant. Be polite when you order them!

1.

tacos

2.

enchiladas

3.

una tostada

Cultura

Foods of the Hispanic World

It is fascinating to learn what people eat around the world. The products that are available in the area where people live influence what they eat.

The long coast of Chile makes seafood an important part of the Chilean diet. High in the Andes where it is difficult to grow vegetables and raise animals, many dishes are made from potatoes.

 Spanish Online

For more information about food in the Spanish-speaking world, go to the Glencoe Web site: **glencoe.com**

In Argentina, people eat more beef than any other country in the world. There are many cattle ranches on the vast Argentine *pampas*.

Corn and corn products are a staple in the diet of many Mexicans. Many dishes are prepared with corn tortillas. In Cuba, the Dominican Republic, and Puerto Rico people eat a lot of rice, beans, and different types of bananas called *plátanos*.

6 ◆ La hora

Telling Time

To find out the time, you ask:

Perdón, ¿qué hora es?

To tell the time, you say:

Es la una.

Son las dos.

Son las tres.

Son las cuatro.

Son las cinco.

Son las seis.

Son las siete.

Son las ocho.

Son las nueve.

Son las diez.

Son las once.

Son las doce.

Es la una y cinco.	**Son las dos y diez.**	**Son las cinco cuarenta.**	**Son las seis y cuarto (y quince).**	**Son las siete y media (y treinta).**

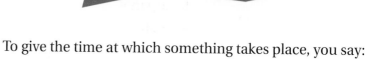

To give the time at which something takes place, you say:

La clase es a las ocho y media (a las ocho y treinta).

El concierto es a las siete y media (a las siete y treinta).

World Youth Orchestra,
Girona, Spain

Actividades

A Walk up to a classmate and ask for the time. Your classmate will answer you.

B Tell at what time you have the following classes. Note that these words are cognates. They are very similar in both Spanish and English.

La clase de matemáticas es...

1. matemáticas
2. historia
3. educación física
4. ciencias
5. español
6. inglés

C Draw pictures of some of your daily activities such as getting up in the morning, eating breakfast, walking or riding the bus to school, going to after-school sports, eating dinner, going to bed, etc. Then compare your pictures with those of a classmate. Both of you will tell when you do these activities. Keep track of how many activities you both do at the same time.

Cultura

The 24-Hour Clock

In Spain and in many areas of Latin America, it is common to use the 24-hour clock for formal activities such as reservations, train and airplane departures. Can you tell what time it is below in English?

A las dieciocho horas

A las veinte cuarenta

In most of the Spanish-speaking countries it is not considered rude to arrive a bit late for an appointment. If you have a 10:00 A.M. appointment, you would be expected sometime between 10 and 10:15.

Look at the Spanish train schedule below. What do you notice about the times?

HORARIOS

MADRID Puerta de Atocha • CIUDAD REAL • PUERTOLLANO • CORDOBA • SEVILLA Santa Justa

	VALLE	LLANO	PUNTA	LLANO	LLANO	LLANO	PUNTA	LLANO	LLANO	LLANO	LLANO	PUNTA	LLANO	LLANO	LLANO
NUMERO DE TREN	9614	9664 (1) (*)	9616 (*)	9618	9622	9624 (1) (*)	9628	9630 (1) (*)	9632	9634 (1) (*)	9636	9638 (1) (*)	9640	9642 (1) (*)	9644 (2)
OBSERVACIONES DIAS DE CIRCULACION	LMXJVSD	LMXJV••	LMXJVS•	LMXJVSD	LMXJVSD	LMXJV••	LMXJVSD	LMXJV••	LMXJVSD	LMXJV•D	LMXJVSD	LMXJV•D	LMXJVSD	LMXJV•D	••••VS•
MADRID Puerta de Atocha	07:00	07:30	08:00	09:00	11:00	12:00	14:00	15:00	16:00	17:00	18:00	19:00	20:00	21:00	22:00
CIUDAD REAL	07:51	08:19		09:49					16:49				20:49		
PUERTOLLANO	08:08	08:35		10:05					17:05				21:05		
CORDOBA	08:57	09:22		10:52	12:44	13:41	15:41	16:41	17:52	18:44	19:44	20:44	21:52	22:44	23:41
SEVILLA Santa Justa	09:40	10:05	10:15	11:35	13:30	14:25	16:25	17:25	18:35	19:30	20:30	21:30	22:35	23:30	00:25
RESTAURACION															

SEVILLA Santa Justa • CORDOBA • PUERTOLLANO • CIUDAD REAL • MADRID Puerta de Atocha

	VALLE	LLANO	PUNTA	LLANO	LLANO	LLANO	LLANO	PUNTA	LLANO	LLANO	LLANO	LLANO	PUNTA	LLANO	LLANO	LLANO
NUMERO DE TREN	9663 (1) (*)	9615	9617 (*)	9619	9621 (3) (*)	9623	9625 (3) (*)	9629	9631 (4) (*)	9633	9635 (1) (*)	9637	9639 (1) (*)	9641	9643 (1) (*)	9645 (5)
OBSERVACIONES DIAS DE CIRCULACION	LMXJV••	LMXJVSD	LMXJVS•	LMXJVSD	LMXJV••	LMXJVSD	LMXJV••	LMXJVSD	••••V••	LMXJVSD	LMXJV•D	LMXJVSD	LMXJV•D	LMXJVSD	LMXJV•D	••••SD
SEVILLA Santa Justa	06:30	07:00	08:00	09:00	10:00	11:00	12:00	14:00	15:00	16:00	17:00	18:00	19:00	20:00	21:00	22:00
CORDOBA	07:13	07:43		09:43	10:43	11:43	12:43	14:43	15:43	16:43	17:43	18:43	19:43	20:43	21:43	22:43
PUERTOLLANO		08:27		10:27						17:25				21:25		
CIUDAD REAL		08:43		10:43						17:42				21:42		
MADRID Puerta de Atocha	08:55	09:40	10:15	11:40	12:25	13:30	14:25	16:25	17:30	18:35	19:30	20:30	21:30	22:35	23:30	00:25
RESTAURACION																

7 · Los colores

Identifying Colors

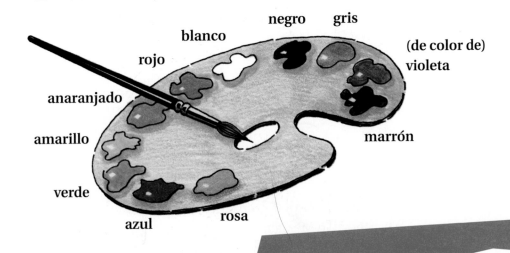

negro gris

blanco

rojo (de color de)
violeta

anaranjado

amarillo marrón

verde

azul rosa

Actividades

A **Give the following information in Spanish.**

1. your favorite color
2. your least favorite color
3. the color of your pencil
4. the color of the sky today
5. the colors you like for clothes

Villahermosa, Mexico

B   **What do you know about color combinations? Complete the following in Spanish.**

1. Los colores rojo y azul combinados hacen el color _____.
2. Los colores azul y amarillo combinados hacen el color _____.
3. Los colores rojo y amarillo combinados hacen el color _____.
4. Los colores negro y blanco combinados hacen el color _____.

C   **Draw a classmate. Use crayons to color his or her clothing. Say what colors he or she is wearing in Spanish.**

Cultura

Pablo Picasso

Pablo Picasso is one of the world's most famous modern artists. He was born in Málaga, Spain, in 1881. His mother claimed that Picasso could draw before he could talk. His father was an art teacher at the famous Barcelona Institute of Fine Arts. Pablo wished to enroll in this school. The entrance exam was so difficult that it often took students a month to complete. Picasso took the exam in one day! He was immediately admitted to the advanced classes.

As with many famous artists, Picasso's work went through many different periods or stages. Some of his periods are given the names of colors. The paintings of his "Blue Period" have a deep, dark blue background. They depicted scenes of loneliness, poverty, and suffering.

A "Pink Period" followed his "Blue Period." Picasso was happier during this time. He painted scenes of acrobats and circus performers in warm, rose-colored hues.

Which painting is from Picasso's "Pink Period"? Which painting is from his "Blue Period"?

The Blind Man's Meal,
Pablo Picasso

Tightrope Walker's Family,
Pablo Picasso

Los días de la semana

Telling the Days of the Week

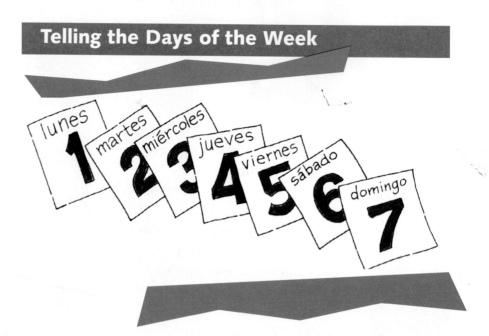

lunes 1 martes 2 miércoles 3 jueves 4 viernes 5 sábado 6 domingo 7

To find out and give the day, you say:

—¿Qué día es hoy?

—Hoy es lunes.

Actividad

A **Answer the following questions in Spanish.**

1. ¿Qué día es hoy?
2. ¿Y mañana?
3. ¿Cuáles son los días del fin de semana o *weekend*?

Cultura

Weekends and Holidays

In many Spanish-speaking countries the meaning of weekend is different from that in the United States. Many people work on Saturdays and some schools have classes on Saturday mornings. Most people do not work on Sundays. Schools are also closed. Sunday is considered a day of rest.

There are many holidays in the Spanish-speaking world. People do not work on holidays. This makes it easier to go to work on Saturdays. Soon there will be another holiday to enjoy!

Spring fair, Jerez de la Frontera, Seville, Spain

Hispanic family, Austin, Texas

Los meses y las estaciones

Telling the Months

ENERO	FEBRERO	MARZO	ABRIL	MAYO	JUNIO
1 2 3 4 5 6 7 8 9 10 11 12 13 14 15 16 17 18 19 20 21 22 23 24 25 26 27 28 29 30 31	1 2 3 4 5 6 7 8 9 10 11 12 13 14 15 16 17 18 19 20 21 22 23 24 25 26 27 28	1 2 3 4 5 6 7 8 9 10 11 12 13 14 15 16 17 18 19 20 21 22 23 24 25 26 27 28 29 30 31	1 2 3 4 5 6 7 8 9 10 11 12 13 14 15 16 17 18 19 20 21 22 23 24 25 26 27 28 29 30	1 2 3 4 5 6 7 8 9 10 11 12 13 14 15 16 17 18 19 20 21 22 23 24 25 26 27 28 29 30 31	1 2 3 4 5 6 7 8 9 10 11 12 13 14 15 16 17 18 19 20 21 22 23 24 25 26 27 28 29 30

JULIO	AGOSTO	SEPTIEMBRE	OCTUBRE	NOVIEMBRE	DICIEMBRE
1 2 3 4 5 6 7 8 9 10 11 12 13 14 15 16 17 18 19 20 21 22 23 24 25 26 27 28 29 30 31	1 2 3 4 5 6 7 8 9 10 11 12 13 14 15 16 17 18 19 20 21 22 23 24 25 26 27 28 29 30 31	1 2 3 4 5 6 7 8 9 10 11 12 13 14 15 16 17 18 19 20 21 22 23 24 25 26 27 28 29 30	1 2 3 4 5 6 7 8 9 10 11 12 13 14 15 16 17 18 19 20 21 22 23 24 25 26 27 28 29 30 31	1 2 3 4 5 6 7 8 9 10 11 12 13 14 15 16 17 18 19 20 21 22 23 24 25 26 27 28 29 30	1 2 3 4 5 6 7 8 9 10 11 12 13 14 15 16 17 18 19 20 21 22 23 24 25 26 27 28 29 30 31

Telling the Seasons

la primavera

el verano

58 • *Welcome to Spanish!*

el otoño

el invierno

Finding Out and Giving the Date

Primero is used for the first of the month. For the other days, you use: *dos, tres, cuatro,* etc. For example, *el dos de mayo.*

—¿Cuál es la fecha de hoy?

—Hoy es martes, el primero de abril.

Actividades

A Each of you will stand up in class and give the date of your birthday in Spanish. Listen and keep a record of how many of you were born in the same month.

B Based on the information from *Actividad A,* tell in Spanish in which month most of the students in the class were born. Tell in which month the fewest were born.

C Work in groups of two or three. Each group is responsible for drawing a calendar for one month of the year. Include the dates of classmates' birthdays.

D In which season of the year is . . . ?

1. mayo
2. enero
3. julio
4. octubre

Cultura

Hispanic Fiestas

Many fiestas of Hispanic origin are celebrated in the United States.

El Día de los Muertos or All Saints' Day, which is celebrated on *el primero* or *el dos de noviembre,* is the Mexican version of Halloween. Mexican Americans decorate their homes with *esqueletos* that symbolize the spirits of the dead. They often go to the cemetery and take food and flowers to those who have departed from this world.

El Cinco de Mayo is celebrated in Mexico to commemorate a military victory by Mexican troops against the French in the city of Puebla in 1862. *El Cinco de Mayo* is also celebrated in the United States. Many think they are celebrating Mexican Independence Day. But *el Día de la Independencia* is celebrated *el dieciséis de septiembre.*

There are many feasts and parades to celebrate national origins. In New York, the Puerto Rican Day parade and the Dominican Day parade are festive events. Marching bands follow beautifully decorated floats up Fifth Avenue.

Describing the Weather

—¿Qué tiempo hace hoy?
—Hace buen tiempo.
  El sol brilla.
  Hay sol. (Hace sol.)

—Hace mal tiempo.
  Está lloviendo.

Hace viento.

Hace calor.

Está nevando.

Hace frío.

Actividades

A Tell in Spanish what the weather is like today.

B Work in groups of four. Write in Spanish the name of each season on a separate sheet of paper. Put the papers in a pile. Each of you will pull one sheet from the pile. Then describe the weather during the season written on the sheet.

C Draw a picture of your favorite type of weather. Then describe your picture to the class in Spanish.

Cultura

Seasons in Latin America

In many Latin-American countries there are only two seasons: *el verano* and *el invierno*. *El verano* is the dry season and *el invierno* is the rainy season.

In South America the seasons are reversed. When it is winter in North America, it is summer in South America. In Chile and Argentina people ski in July and go to the beach in January! Why do you think that the seasons are reversed?

Mar del Plata, Argentina

"La Hoya," ski center in Esquel, Argentina

11 Yo soy...

Telling Who I Am

—¡Hola! ¿Quién eres?

—¿Yo? (Yo) soy Juan Gutiérrez. Y tú, ¿quién eres?

—(Yo) soy Anita Salas.

When you hear a question with *eres* in Spanish, you answer with *soy. Eres* is used to speak to a friend *(tú)* and *soy* is used to speak about yourself *(yo).*

¿eres? → **soy**

Actividades

A Walk around the classroom. Greet each of your classmates. Find out who each one is. Let each one know who you are.

B Turn to your nearest neighbor. Have a conversation with him or her. Use the following as your guide.

—¡Hola! ¿Quién eres?

  —¿Quién? ¿Yo?

—Sí, tú.

  —Pues, yo soy _____. Y tú, ¿quién eres?

—Soy _____.

Cultura

Names in Spanish

Some Spanish speakers use two last names. A young person, prior to marriage, uses the family name of both his or her father and mother. For example,

María Eugenia Guzmán Morales.

Guzmán is the name of María Eugenia's father's family and Morales is the name of her mother's family.

12 ◆ *Soy de...*

Telling Where I Am From

—¿De dónde eres, David?

—Soy de Dallas.

—Ah, eres americano.

—Sí, soy americano. ¿Y tú? ¿De dónde eres, Anita?

—Soy de Guadalajara. Soy mexicana.

When you describe a boy in Spanish, you use -*o*. When you describe a girl in Spanish, you use -*a*.

David es americano.

Yo soy americano.

Anita es mexicana.

Yo soy mexicana.

Actividades

A Answer the following questions about yourself.

1. ¿Quién eres?
2. ¿De dónde eres?
3. ¿De qué nacionalidad eres?

B Draw a picture of a male friend or relative. Give him a Spanish name. Then tell as much about him as you can.

C Draw a picture of a female friend or relative. Give her a Spanish name. Then tell as much about her as you can.

D Work with a classmate. Find out where he or she is from and his or her nationality. Then give your classmate the same information about yourself.

Conversando más

—¡Hola!
 —¡Hola!
—¿Quién eres?
 —Pues, yo soy David Sanders.
—¿Qué tal, David?
 —Muy bien. ¿Y tú?
—Bien, gracias.
 —Tú eres Anita Salas, ¿no?
—Sí, soy Anita.
 —¿De dónde eres, Anita?
—Soy de México.
 —Ah, eres mexicana.
—Sí. Y tú eres americano, ¿no?
 —Sí, soy de Dallas.

Actividades

A   Practice the conversation on page 67 together with a class-mate. Use as much expression as you can. One will read the part of David and the other will read the part of Anita.

B   Complete the following story about David and Anita.

David es de _____, Tejas. David es _____. No es mexicano. _____ es de México. Es de Guadalajara. Anita no es _____. Anita es _____.

C   Look at the photograph of Lynn Smith. She is from New Jersey. Tell all about her in Spanish.

D   Look at this photograph of José Garza. He is from Monterrey, Mexico. Tell all about him in Spanish.

Cultura
Nationalities

People from all countries of North America, Central America, and South America are *americanos.* The term *americano* (sometimes *norteamericano*) is more frequently used, however, for citizens of the United States. The term *estadounidense* is not often heard to refer to the nationality of a person. People from other countries of the Americas usually identify themselves more specifically as *colombiano, argentino, mexicano.* Do you know people from these countries?

School celebration, Mexico City

Centennial parade, Pasto, Colombia

High school class, Argentina

12 · *Soy de...* • 69

13 Hablo español

Telling What I Speak

—¿Hablas inglés, David?

—Sí, hablo inglés. ¿Hablas español, Anita?

—Sí, hablo español.

—¿Hablas inglés también?

—Sí, hablo inglés también.

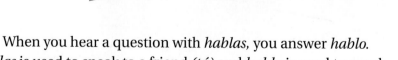

When you hear a question with *hablas,* you answer *hablo.*
Hablas is used to speak to a friend *(tú)* and *hablo* is used to speak
about yourself *(yo).*

¿hablas? → **hablo**

Look at the Spanish names of these languages. You can probably guess at the meaning as all of these words are cognates.

italiano	ruso
francés	polaco
portugués	árabe
chino	griego
japonés	latín

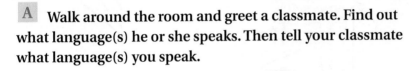

What languages are taught at this school in Colombia?

Actividades

A Walk around the room and greet a classmate. Find out what language(s) he or she speaks. Then tell your classmate what language(s) you speak.

B Get a beach ball. One person throws the ball to another as he or she asks, *¿Hablas español?* The person who catches the ball answers, *Sí, hablo...* or *No, no hablo...*

C If you speak a language other than English at home, tell the class what language you speak.

Cultura

Spanish in the World

Spanish is the official language of more countries in the world than any other language. It is the language of more than twenty countries. However, it is not the language with the most speakers. Do you know which language is spoken by the largest number of people in the world? The answer is Chinese. Chinese is spoken by more than one billion people!

One of the largest cities in the world is also a Spanish-speaking city. Mexico City has a population of approximately 8.5 million inhabitants. Mexico City, along with Shanghai and Tokyo, rates among the largest cities in the world.

Mexico City, Mexico

Tokyo, Japan

Shanghai, China

14 ◆ E *studio...*

—David, ¿estudias español en la escuela?

—Sí, estudio español. Y tú, ¿qué lengua estudias en la escuela?

—Estudio inglés.

Actividades

A Get a beach ball. One person throws the ball to another as he or she asks, *¿Estudias español?* The person who catches the ball answers, *Sí, estudio...* or *No, no estudio...*

B Work with a classmate. Find out what you each study in school. You can easily guess at the meaning of the words you'll need.

español	ciencias	arte
inglés	historia	música
matemáticas	geografía	educación física

C Tell a classmate about one of your classes—math, for example. Use the following questions as a guide.

1. ¿Estudias matemáticas?
2. ¿Cómo es el curso de matemáticas? ¿Es interesante?
3. ¿Quién es el profesor o la profesora de matemáticas?
4. ¿A qué hora es la clase de matemáticas?

When you talk about someone, you say *estudia* or *habla*.

David habla inglés pero estudia español en la escuela.

Anita habla español y estudia inglés en la escuela.

Actividades

A **Read the following story about David and Anita.**

David es americano. Es de Dallas. David habla inglés. En la escuela él estudia español. Toma un curso de español.

Anita es mexicana. Es de Guadalajara. Anita habla español. En la escuela ella estudia inglés. Toma un curso de inglés en la escuela.

B **Work with a classmate. One of you will ask questions about David and the other will answer the questions. Then you'll switch parts for the questions about Anita.**

Estudiante A

1. ¿De qué nacionalidad es David?
2. ¿Qué lengua habla?
3. ¿Qué estudia?
4. ¿Dónde toma un curso de español?

Estudiante B

1. ¿De qué nacionalidad es Anita?
2. ¿Qué lengua habla?
3. ¿Qué estudia?
4. ¿Dónde toma un curso de inglés?

C **Answer the following questions about yourself.**

1. ¿Quién eres?
2. ¿De dónde eres?
3. ¿Qué lengua hablas?
4. ¿Qué lengua estudias en la escuela?

Cultura

Education in Spain and Latin America

In many schools of Spain and Latin America classes do not meet every day. The students' schedules vary from day-to-day. Many subjects meet three times a week, for example. For this reason students take more subjects per semester than do American students.

Chemistry class, Colombia

15 ◆ Mi casa

el cuarto de baño

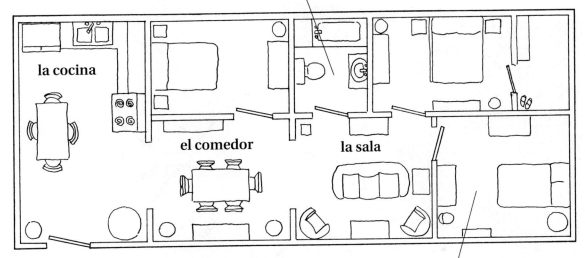

la cocina

el comedor

la sala

el apartamento

el cuarto de dormir
(el dormitorio, la recámara)

el garaje

el carro

el jardín

la casa

una casa pequeña

Hay means "there is" or "there are" in Spanish:

Hay un jardín alrededor de la casa.

Hay un carro en el garaje.

Hay seis cuartos en la casa. Es una casa grande.

Actividades

A Draw a picture of your house. Write the title *Mi casa* at the top of your drawing. Then answer the following questions.

1. ¿Es grande o pequeña tu casa?
2. ¿Cuántos cuartos hay en tu casa?
3. ¿Hay un jardín alrededor de tu casa?

B Look at these photographs of the interiors of houses in Spanish-speaking countries. Give the name in Spanish for each room.

C Describe your dream house to a classmate. Say as much as you can about it in Spanish.

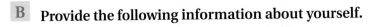

Actividades

A Look at the address book below and give the following information.

1. la dirección de la señorita Gómez
2. el número de teléfono de la señorita Gómez

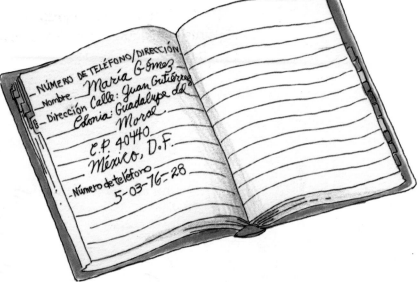

B Provide the following information about yourself.

1. mi dirección
2. mi número de teléfono

16 ◆ Mi familia

Describing My Family

mi abuela   mi abuelo

mi tío   mi tía

mi madre   mi padre

mi prima   mi primo

mi hermano   yo   mi hermana

Mi tío Carlos es el hermano de mi padre.

Mi tía Antonia es la hermana de mi madre.

Mi prima Lupita es la hija de mi tío Carlos.

Mi primo Luis es el hijo de mi tío Juan.

—¿Tienes un hermano?

   —Sí, tengo un hermano. (o) No, no tengo un hermano.

—¿Tienes una familia grande o pequeña?

   —Yo tengo una familia _____. Hay _____ personas en mi familia.

When you hear a question with *tienes* in Spanish, you answer with *tengo. (Tú) tienes* is used to speak to a friend. *Tengo* is used to speak about yourself *(yo)*.

   ¿tienes? → **tengo**

Actividades

A   **Answer the following questions about your family.**

1. ¿Tienes una familia grande o pequeña?
2. ¿Tienes hermanos?
3. ¿Cuántos hermanos tienes?
4. ¿Cuántas personas hay en tu familia?
5. ¿Cuántos cuartos hay en tu casa?

B   **Work with a classmate. Ask each other questions about your families in Spanish.**

C   **Who is it? Answer in Spanish.**

1. la hija de mi padre
2. el hijo de mi madre
3. el hermano de mi madre
4. la madre de mi padre
5. el padre de mi madre
6. la hija de mi tío

Con profundo amor
para mi Madre
EN SU CUMPLEAÑOS

AGC, Inc. Reprinted with Permission.

When you talk about someone, you use *tiene.*

Mi amigo José tiene una familia grande.

Él tiene seis hermanos.

Actividad

A Look at the photograph of *la familia González.* Say as much as you can about the family in Spanish.

Telling Age

To tell how old you or someone else is, you say:

Yo tengo doce años.

Mi hermana tiene quince años.

To ask how old someone is, you say:

¿Cuántos años tienes?

Actividades

A Ask each of your classmates his or her age. Tell each one your age.

B Give the ages of some of your friends and relatives.

Cultura

The Family in Hispanic Culture

La familia is an extremely important unit in all Spanish-speaking cultures. The family gets together to celebrate the major holidays, as well as all personal events such as birthdays, baptisms, anniversaries, etc. In addition to the parents and children, the extended Hispanic family often includes grandparents, uncles, aunts, distant cousins, and godparents.

Especialmente Para Ti
EN TU CUMPLEAÑOS

AGC, Inc. Reprinted with Permission.

17 ▷ Mi *mascota*

Talking About My Pet

los pájaros

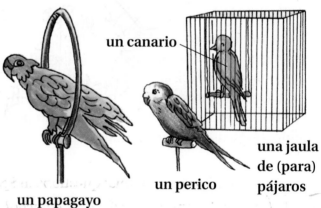

un canario

un perro

un papagayo

un perico

una jaula de (para) pájaros

un gato

un pececillo   un pez dorado

un hámster

un gerbo

un pecero, un acuario

Telling What I Like

—¿Te interesan los animales?

—Sí, los animales me interesan mucho.

Me encantan los animales.

Me fascinan.

Me gustan mucho.

—¿Te gusta tu perro?

—Sí, me gusta mucho.

Actividades

A **Answer the following personal questions in Spanish.**

1. ¿Te encantan los animales? ¿Te gustan mucho?

2. ¿Tienes un perro o un gato? ¿Te gusta tu perro o tu gato?

3. ¿Te encantan los pájaros? ¿Te gustan mucho? ¿Tienes un pájaro? ¿Qué tipo de pájaro tienes?

4. ¿Te encantan los peces? ¿Te gustan mucho? ¿Tienes peces? ¿Qué tipo de pez tienes?

B **Ask a classmate all about his or her pet. Use the following questions as a guide.**

1. ¿Tienes una mascota?

2. ¿Qué tienes?

3. ¿Tiene nombre?

4. ¿Cuántos años (meses) tiene?

5. ¿Es adorable?

Boy with pet llama, Cuzco, Peru

Telling What My Pet Does

**El perro ladra. Ladra y salta.
Juega mucho.**

**El gato maúlla. El gato salta y
juega mucho también.**

**El pececillo nada
en el pecero (acuario).**

El papagayo habla.

**El canario canta
en su jaula.**

Actividades

A   **Tell if the following animals or pets play.**

1. el pez dorado
2. el perro
3. el papagayo
4. el hámster
5. el gato

B   **Match the name of the animal with what it does.**

1. un pájaro   a. habla
2. un perro   b. salta
3. un gato   c. canta
4. un pez   d. nada
5. un gerbo   e. juega
6. un canario   f. ladra
7. un hámster   g. maúlla
8. un papagayo

C If you have a pet, bring a photograph of your pet to class or draw a picture. Tell your classmates about your pet in Spanish.

Cultura

Pets

Until recently, families living in the cities of Spain and Latin America tended not to have pets. Animals were considered better off on a farm. Today, however, many families are acquiring pets, particularly in the more wealthy metropolitan areas. *El perrito* is usually the preferred pet.

Every language has its imitations for animal sounds. In English, we say a dog goes "woof, woof" and a cat goes "meow." Let's see what the Spanish animals say:

el perro: "jau, jau"   **el gallo:** "quiquiriquí"

el gato: "miau, miau"   **la oveja:** "be, be"

la vaca: "mu, mu"

18 ◆ *Los deportes*

Sports

el campo

el equipo

el béisbol

el balón

el vólibol

el fútbol

la pelota

la cancha

el tenis

el jugador

la jugadora

el básquetbol, el baloncesto

—Antonio, ¿juegas fútbol?

—Sí, juego fútbol.

—¿Juegas con el equipo de la escuela?

—Sí, es un equipo muy bueno.

Actividades

A Write a list of the sports that you enjoy playing.

Juego...

Me gusta...

B Get a beach ball. One student throws the ball to another. The one who throws the ball asks a question with *¿Juegas...?* The one who catches the ball answers with *Sí, juego...* or *No, no juego...*

C Answer the following personal questions.

1. ¿Te interesan los deportes?
2. ¿Te gustan mucho?
3. ¿Qué deporte te gusta más? ¿Cuál es tu deporte favorito?
4. ¿Juegas con el equipo de la escuela?
5. ¿Es bueno el equipo?

D Give the following information about your favorite sport.

1. ¿Cuál es tu deporte favorito?
2. ¿Es un deporte de equipo?
3. ¿Cuántos jugadores hay en el equipo?
4. ¿Juegas _____?
5. ¿Juegas _____ con un balón o con una pelota?

E Here's a photograph of a German team, "VFE Stuttgart" playing a Spanish team, "Espanyol" in Barcelona, Spain. Say as much about the photograph as you can.

Cultura

Sports in the Spanish-Speaking World

Sports are very popular in Spain and Latin America, particularly *fútbol*. However, it is not very common for schools to have organized sports teams. Competition between schools (intermural sports) is almost unheard of. Intramural sports are more popular. There are many local sports clubs which compete, mainly in *fútbol*. The *fútbol* played in Spain and Latin America is soccer, not American football.

Marathon, Mexico City

Field hockey team, Argentina

19 La ropa

Clothing

la camisa

los **el** pantalón,es
un pantalón largo

el gorro

la falda

los zapatos

la camiseta

la blusa

la sudadera

la chaqueta,
el saco

un pantalón es
corto es

los shorts

los tenis

el blue jean es

Actividades

A In Spanish, tell what you are wearing today.

Llevo...

B Talk about the dress code in your school. Use the following questions as a guide.

1. ¿Llevan uniforme a la escuela los alumnos?
2. ¿Llevan blue jeans los muchachos y las muchachas?
3. ¿Llevan los alumnos una sudadera en la clase de educación física?
4. ¿Llevan los alumnos tenis a la escuela?

Cultura

Clothing Today

The clothing usually worn by young people today in many parts of Spain and Latin America is the same as the clothing you wear. But there are also many interesting and different local clothing styles worn for *fiestas*.

Santiago, Chile

Mexico City, Mexico

Welcome to *French!*

French, like Spanish, is a Romance language. It also comes from Latin. French is a beautiful language spoken on many continents of the world. It is also the second language of many people. To speak French is considered the sign of an educated person in many parts of the world.

French is spoken by some 125 million people. It is, of course, the official language of France. It is also the language of parts of Belgium and Switzerland, as well as the principality of Monaco. It is widely spoken in Algeria, Morocco, and Tunisia in North Africa. It is also the language used in many other parts of Africa: the Ivory Coast, Mali, Togo, the Democratic Republic of Congo, Senegal, Niger, and Mauritania. French is also spoken in Southeast Asia: Vietnam, Cambodia, Laos, as well as some of the Polynesian islands of the Pacific.

Closer to home, French is the language of Martinique, Guadeloupe, and Haiti in the Caribbean. It is also the language of Quebec, Canada. Because New England is so close to Quebec, there are many families of French Canadian background living in New England. The state of Louisiana received its name from the famous French king, Louis XIV. There is still much French influence in Louisiana.

Nice, France

Provence, France

Toulouse

Notre-Dame Cathedral,
Paris, France

Rocher du Diamant,
Martinique

French to English

Many words have come into the English language from French. Do you recognize any of them?

à la carte
avenue
ballet
Bon voyage!
cabaret

cuisine
façade
hors d'oeuvre
soupe du jour
vogue

1 **L***es salutations*

Greeting People

—Salut, Philippe.
　—Salut, Émilie. Ça va?
—Ça va. Et toi?
　—Ça va bien, merci.

In French-speaking countries, young people usually shake hands when they meet. Pretend that you are in France and shake hands with your classmates as you greet them.

Activités

A Get up from your desk and walk around the classroom. Say "hi" in French to each classmate you meet. Don't forget to shake hands.

B Work in groups of two. Make up a little conversation in French. Greet each other and find out how things are going.

Bonjour is a more formal greeting than *salut*. You would say *bonjour* when greeting adults, for example. You would also use the person's title with *bonjour*:

Bonjour, Monsieur.

Bonjour, Madame.

Bonjour, Mademoiselle.

In French, people say *Bonjour, Monsieur* or *Bonjour, Madame*. They do not use the person's name with the title. What do we say in English?

When you want to find out how things are going, you ask:

Ça va?

There are many different responses to *Ça va?* Some common ones are:

Ça va, merci.

Oui, ça va.

Ça va bien, merci.

Bien, merci.

Pas mal. Et toi?

Pont Alexandre, Paris, France

Do you know what this candy wrapper says?

Activités

A   Draw and cut out five stick figures. Give each one a name. They will represent your friends, family, and teachers. Greet each of your stick figures properly in French.

B   Work with a classmate. Make up a conversation in French. Greet each other and find out how things are going. Then pretend one of you is a teacher and make the necessary changes.

C   Look at these photographs of people greeting each other in Lyon, France. Do they do some of the things we do when they greet each other? Do they do some things that are different? Explain.

2 Au revoir

Saying "Good-bye"

—Au revoir, Didier.
—Au revoir, Nathalie.

—Ciao, Christian.
—Ciao, Catherine.
 À tout à l'heure!

The usual expression to use when saying "good-bye" to someone is:

Au revoir.

If you plan to see the person again quite soon, you can say:

À bientôt.

À tout à l'heure.

If you plan to see the person the next day, you can say:

À demain.

An informal way to say "good-bye" that you frequently hear is:

Ciao!

Ciao is an Italian expression that is used in several other European languages.

Activités

A Go over to a classmate. Say "so long" to him or her and then return to your seat. Don't forget to use his or her French name.

B Work with a friend in class. Say *ciao* to one another and let each other know that you'll be getting together again soon.

C Say "good-bye" to your teacher in French and then say "good-bye" to a friend. Use a different term with each person!

Récapitulons!

—Salut, Pierre.

   —Salut, Martine. Ça va?

—Oui, ça va. Et toi?

   —Pas mal, merci.

—Ciao, Pierre.

   —Au revoir, Martine. À demain.

Activités

A Work with a friend. Speak French together. Have fun saying as much as you can to each other!

B Look at these photographs of people saying "good-bye" in Guadeloupe and France. Describe what the people are doing.

Culture

Common First Names

The following are some common names for boys and girls in French.

Garçons

Alain, Albert, Bruno, Bernard, Charles, Christian, Denis, Éric, Eugène, François, Georges, Guy, Henri, Jean, Joseph, Louis, Marcel, Nicolas, Patrice, Paul, René, Richard, Sébastien, Serge, Thierry, Thomas, Victor, Xavier, Yves

Jeunes filles

Adèle, Anne, Bernadette, Brigitte, Catherine, Chantal, Danielle, Dominique, Émilie, Ève, Françoise, Gabrielle, Germaine, Hélène, Isabelle, Jacqueline, Jeanne, Lise, Louise, Marie, Nathalie, Pauline, Sara, Thérèse, Valérie

3 En classe

Identifying Classroom Objects

To find out what something is, you ask:

Qu'est-ce que c'est?

une chaise

une feuille de papier

un livre

une table

un ordinateur

un tableau noir

une brosse

un morceau de craie

un cahier

une calculatrice

une gomme   un bloc

un stylo-bille

un crayon

une chaise   un sac à dos

To ask for something in a polite way, you say:

Une feuille de papier, s'il vous plaît.

When speaking to a friend, however, you would say:

Une feuille de papier, s'il te plaît.

Activités

A Ask a classmate for the following items in French. Don't forget to ask politely!

1.
2.
3.
4.
5.
6.

B Look again at the drawings in Activité A. Pretend you are the student and ask your teacher for what you need. Be polite!

C Look at each picture below and say in French what each person needs.

1.
2.

3.

4.

D Point out a classroom object and ask a classmate what it is.

Culture

Schools in France

In France, a middle school is called *un collège*. Students attend *un collège* for four years. They then go on to high school, *un lycée*. The last year of high school is called *la terminale*. At the end of *la terminale*, students take a very difficult exam called *le baccalauréat*. Students call it *le bac*. A student who passes *le bac* can enter any university in France.

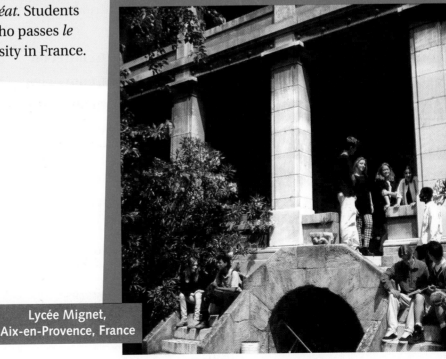

Lycée Mignet,
Aix-en-Provence, France

4 ◆ Les nombres

Counting in French

1	un	21	vingt et un	40	quarante
2	deux	22	vingt-deux	50	cinquante
3	trois	23	vingt-trois	60	soixante
4	quatre	24	vingt-quatre	70	soixante-dix
5	cinq	25	vingt-cinq	80	quatre-vingts
6	six	26	vingt-six	90	quatre-vingt-dix
7	sept	27	vingt-sept		
8	huit	28	vingt-huit	100	cent
9	neuf	29	vingt-neuf	200	deux cents
10	dix	30	trente	300	trois cents
				400	quatre cents
11	onze	31	trente et un	500	cinq cents
12	douze	32	trente-deux	600	six cents
13	treize	33	trente-trois	700	sept cents
14	quatorze	34	trente-quatre	800	huit cents
15	quinze	35	trente-cinq	900	neuf cents
16	seize	36	trente-six	1.000	mille
17	dix-sept	37	trente-sept		
18	dix-huit	38	trente-huit		
19	dix-neuf	39	trente-neuf		
20	vingt				

Activités

A Your teacher will write some numbers on the chalkboard. Then he or she will call out the number in French and ask a student to circle the correct number.

B Work with a classmate. One of you will count from 30 to 40. The other will count from 70 to 80.

C Have a contest with a friend. See who can count the fastest from 1 to 100 by tens.

D Have a contest with a friend. See who can count the fastest from 100 to 1000 by hundreds.

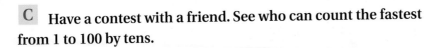

Finding Out the Price

To find out how much something costs, you ask:

—S'il vous plaît, Madame. C'est combien le stylo-bille?

—Huit euros.

—Merci, Madame.

Note the following differences when writing numbers in English and French:

anglais	français
24.90	24,90
1,000	1.000
2:40	2^{h}40

Activité

A Work with a classmate. One of you will be the customer and the other will be the clerk at a stationery store. Make up a conversation to buy the following things.

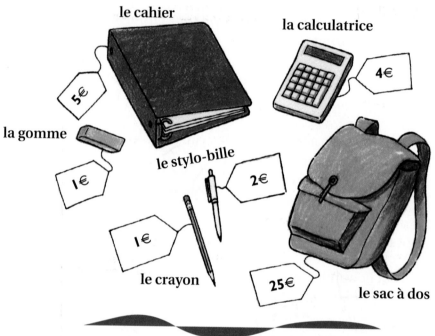

le cahier

la calculatrice

4€

5€

la gomme

le stylo-bille

1€

2€

le crayon

1€

25€

le sac à dos

Culture

French Money

The monetary unit in France is the euro.

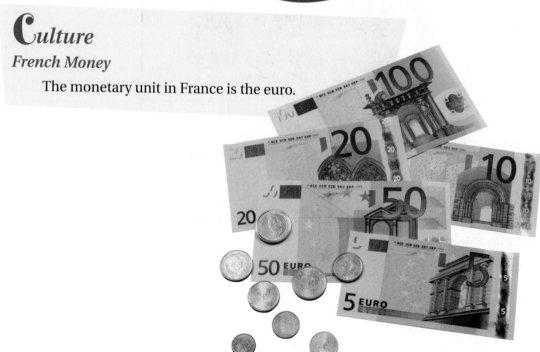

Activité

A Give the price of each item from the clothing store ad.

REVUE DE DETAILS

NEWS MODE

Repéré aux quatre coins de la mode, tout ce qui nous plaît. De la tête aux pieds.

Coloris: noir, beige.
Tailles: du 36 au 40 pour la femme; du 40 au 45 pour l'homme.

**modèle femme
du 36 au 40**   76,00 €

**modèle homme
du 40 au 45**   76,00 €

l'une
15,00 €

Chemise
77% viscose,
23% polyester.

Coloris assortis.
Du 37/38 au 43/44.

l'une
15,00 €

Cravate
100% soie.
Coloris assortis.

(1) Robe en velours (150 €, 5 tailles, 8 coloris).
(2) Veste sur jupe en taffetas de soie (75 €, 3 tailles, 5 coloris (veste) et 150 €, du 36 au 42, en noir ou bronze (jupe)).

---

1. une chemise
2. une cravate
3. les sandales

4. deux robes
5. trois cravates

5 ◆ **L***a politesse*

—Bonjour. Deux cocas, s'il vous plaît.

(The server brings the order.)
—Merci.
  —Je vous en prie.

(A little later.)
　—C'est combien, s'il vous plaît?
　—Trois euros.

In addition to *je vous en prie,* other ways to express "you're welcome" are:

De rien.

Il n'y a pas de quoi.

In French there is a difference between formal and informal speech. When you are speaking with someone you know well or someone your own age, you would say:

S'il te plaît.

Je t'en prie.

With an adult or someone that you have just met, however, you would say:

S'il vous plaît.

Je vous en prie.

Activités

A With a friend, practice reading the conversation on pages 110–111 aloud.

B You are at a café in the village of St. Rémy de Provence, France. Order the following things. Ask a classmate to be the server.

1. un sandwich

2. un thé

3. un coca

4. une limonade

5. une salade

C You would like to order the following foods at a French restaurant. Be polite when you order them!

1. un steak

2. trois crêpes

3. une tarte aux fruits

une soupe à l'oignon

4.

5. une omelette

D Look at this photograph of French-speaking teenagers from Canada enjoying a snack together. Describe what you see.

Culture

"Fast Food" in Paris

In Paris there are many restaurants that cater to students. These restaurants serve good food at reasonable prices. Many are ethnic restaurants serving Greek, Italian, North African, or Middle Eastern food.

If you are really in a hurry, there are little sandwich and pastry shops where you can get a quick snack and eat on the run. There are also little carts on the street where you can buy a packaged sandwich or salad.

Le temps des semailles

RESTAURANT

15, rue Brueys
AIX EN PROVENCE
TEL. 42.38.38.62
FAX. 42.38.38.62

RESTAURANT
VIÊT - NAM
Spécialités
Vietnamiennes et Chinoises
98, Avenue De Lattre de Tassigny
(Ex. Avenue de la Gare)
04100 MANOSQUE

6 ◆ L'heure

Telling Time

To find out the time, you ask:

Il est quelle heure?

Pardon, vous avez l'heure?

To tell the time, you say:

Il est une heure.

Il est deux heures.

Il est trois heures.

Il est quatre heures.

Il est cinq heures.

Il est six heures.

Il est sept heures.

Il est huit heures.

Il est neuf heures.

Il est dix heures.

Il est onze heures.

Il est douze heures.

116 • *Welcome to French!*

Il est une heure cinq.   **Il est deux heures dix.**   **Il est cinq heures quarante.**   **Il est six heures quinze.**   **Il est sept heures et demie. Il est sept heures trente.**

Activités

A   **Give the following times.**

B Walk up to a classmate and ask for the time. Your classmate will answer you.

Telling at What Time

To ask and tell at what time something takes place, you say:

La classe est *à* **quelle heure?**

La classe est *à* **neuf heures et demie.**

In France, it is common to use the 24-hour clock for formal activities such as reservations, train and plane departures.

À dix-huit heures (18h00)

À vingt heures quarante (20h40)

Activités

A Tell at what time you have the following classes. You will note that these words are cognates. They are similar in both French and English.

1. le cours de maths
2. le cours d'histoire
3. le cours de gymnastique
4. le cours de sciences
5. le cours d'anglais

B Draw pictures of some of your daily activities such as getting up in the morning, eating breakfast, walking or riding the bus to school, going to afternoon sports, eating dinner, going to bed, etc. Then compare your pictures with those of a classmate. Tell at what time each of you does the particular activity. Keep track of how many activities both of you do at the same time.

Culture

Time Zones

It's not the same time in all the countries of the French-speaking world. French is the official or second language in countries that stretch over many different time zones.

Quebec, Canada

During the 19th century, French colonies extended from Asia to the Americas. The French language is still widely spoken in many of these ex-colonies of France.

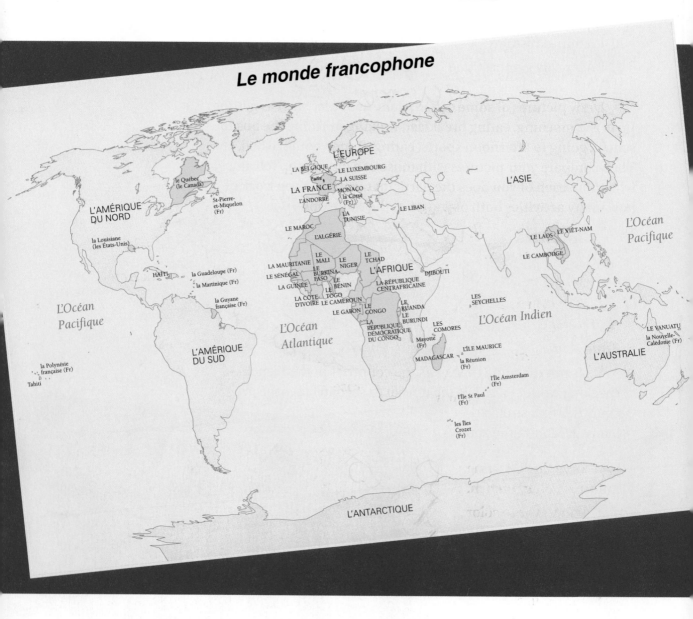

Le monde francophone

7 *Les couleurs*

Identifying Colors

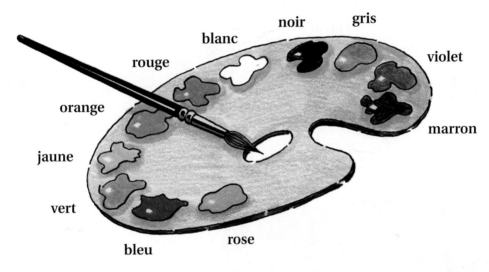

noir
gris
blanc
rouge
violet
orange
marron
jaune
vert
bleu
rose

Activités

A Give the following information in French.

1. your favorite color
2. your least favorite color
3. the colors you like for clothes
4. the color of an apple

Les îles de la Madeleine, Canada

B Draw a classmate. Use crayons to color his or her clothing. Say what colors he or she is wearing in French.

Culture

French Impressionism

Impressionism is a style of painting that started in France during the 1860s. Two leaders of this famous movement were Claude Monet and Pierre Renoir.

The impressionists took their easels, brushes, and paints outdoors to paint rather than work in a studio. They stressed the effects of sunlight on the subject they were painting. They used quick, short brushstrokes and bright colors. This gave the effect of small dabs or dots of paint on the canvas. When you look at an impressionist painting from a distance, these dabs of color blend together and create a beautiful effect.

Look at these paintings by Claude Monet and Berthe Morisot, another French impressionist painter. Tell the colors they use in French.

"The Sisters," 1869
Berthe Morisot

"Banks of the Seine, Vétheuil," 1880
Claude Monet

8 Les jours de la semaine

Telling the Days of the Week

lundi 1 · mardi 2 · mercredi 3 · Jeudi 4 · vendredi 5 · Samedi 6 · dimanche 7

To find out the day, you ask:
—C'est quel jour (aujourd'hui)?
(ou) Quel jour est-ce?

To answer, you say:
—C'est lundi.
(ou) Aujourd'hui c'est lundi.
—Et demain?
—Demain, c'est mardi.

Activités

A   **Answer the following questions in French.**

1. C'est quel jour aujourd'hui?

2. Et demain? C'est quel jour?

3. Quels sont les jours de la fin de semaine (du weekend)?

B   **Work with a partner. One person says a day of the week, the other responds with the next day. Then do just the opposite. One person says the name of the day and the other partner gives the day before it.**

Culture

The French Calendar

The first day of the week on a French calendar is *lundi* and the last day of the week is *dimanche*. How does this compare with American calendars? In France, schools are in session on Saturday mornings. Most schools, however, do not have classes on Wednesday afternoon.

Lycée Mignet
Aix-en-Provence, France

LE MENU DE LA SEMAINE
DU <u>lundi 17 juin</u> AU <u>vendredi 21 juin</u>

LUNDI 17

Maquereux à la moutarde
Cordon bleu
Petits pois à la française
Fromage
Pêche

MARDI 18

Pamplemousse / Sucre
Sauté de bœuf
Pâtes au gruyère
Compote

MERCREDI 19

Tomates mayonnaise
Vol au vent aux fruits
   de mer
Riz au gruyère
Fraises chantilly

JEUDI 20

Salade verte
Jambon
Raviolis
Glace

VENDREDI 21

Salade Niçoise
Poulet rôti aux herbes
Haricots verts au beurr
Fromage
Fruit

9 ◆ *Les mois et les saisons*

Telling the Months

JANVIER	FÉVRIER	MARS	AVRIL	MAI	JUIN
1 2 3 4 5 6 7 8 9 10 11 12 13 14 15 16 17 18 19 20 21 22 23 24 25 26 27 28 29 30 31	1 2 3 4 5 6 7 8 9 10 11 12 13 14 15 16 17 18 19 20 21 22 23 24 25 26 27 28	1 2 3 4 5 6 7 8 9 10 11 12 13 14 15 16 17 18 19 20 21 22 23 24 25 26 27 28 29 30 31	1 2 3 4 5 6 7 8 9 10 11 12 13 14 15 16 17 18 19 20 21 22 23 24 25 26 27 28 29 30	1 2 3 4 5 6 7 8 9 10 11 12 13 14 15 16 17 18 19 20 21 22 23 24 25 26 27 28 29 30 31	1 2 3 4 5 6 7 8 9 10 11 12 13 14 15 16 17 18 19 20 21 22 23 24 25 26 27 28 29 30

JUILLET	AOÛT	SEPTEMBRE	OCTOBRE	NOVEMBRE	DÉCEMBRE
1 2 3 4 5 6 7 8 9 10 11 12 13 14 15 16 17 18 19 20 21 22 23 24 25 26 27 28 29 30 31	1 2 3 4 5 6 7 8 9 10 11 12 13 14 15 16 17 18 19 20 21 22 23 24 25 26 27 28 29 30 31	1 2 3 4 5 6 7 8 9 10 11 12 13 14 15 16 17 18 19 20 21 22 23 24 25 26 27 28 29 30	1 2 3 4 5 6 7 8 9 10 11 12 13 14 15 16 17 18 19 20 21 22 23 24 25 26 27 28 29 30 31	1 2 3 4 5 6 7 8 9 10 11 12 13 14 15 16 17 18 19 20 21 22 23 24 25 26 27 28 29 30	1 2 3 4 5 6 7 8 9 10 11 12 13 14 15 16 17 18 19 20 21 22 23 24 25 26 27 28 29 30 31

Telling the Seasons

au printemps

en été

en automne   en hiver

Finding Out and Giving the Date

—Quelle est la date aujourd'hui?
—Le premier avril.

Premier is used for the first of the month. For the other days, *deux, trois, quatre* are used. For example, *le trois juin*.

Activités

A Draw your own French calendar. Label correctly all the months and days of the week. Do it in the French style.

B Each of you will stand up in class and give your birthday. Listen and keep a record of how many of you were born in each month.

C Based on the information from *Activité B*, tell in French in which month most of the students in the class were born. Tell in which month the fewest were born.

D In which season of the year is . . . ?

1. janvier
2. mai
3. août
4. novembre

Bon anniversaire!

*C*ulture

Vacation Time in France

The month of August is vacation month in France—*les grandes vacances*. Almost all businesses close for the entire month and people leave the cities for the beaches and mountains. Paris and the other major French cities are deserted in August.

Study the photograph on the left. You will see that the beautiful beach at Nice is not sandy. It has stones which are called *galets*.

◆ 10 ◆ L*e temps*

Describing the Weather

—Quel temps fait-il aujourd'hui?

—Il fait très beau.

Il y a du soleil.

—Il fait mauvais.

Il pleut.

Il y a du vent.

Il fait chaud.

Il neige.

Il fait froid.

Activités

A Tell in French what the weather is like today.

B Work in groups of four. Write in French the name of each season on a separate sheet of paper. Put the papers in a pile. Each of you will pull one sheet from the pile and describe the weather of the season written on the sheet.

C Draw a picture of your favorite type of weather. Then describe your picture to the class in French.

Culture

A Special Winter Class

During the winter, French elementary schools offer *classes de neige*. Elementary school students are taken to a winter resort where they learn to ski. In the morning they take their regular school subjects. In the afternoon they have skiing lessons. The *classes de neige* last for about one week.

Isola deux mille, France

11 ◆ *Je suis...*

Telling Who I Am

—Salut! Tu es un ami de Jean-Luc, n'est-ce pas?

—Oui, je suis David Sanders. Et tu es Nathalie, n'est-ce pas?

—Oui, je suis Nathalie Gaudin. Je suis une amie de Jean-Luc.

When you hear the question *tu es?* in French, you answer with *je suis. Tu es* is used to speak to a friend and *je suis* is used to speak about yourself.

tu es? → **je suis**

If you want to find out the name of a person the same age as you, you can ask:

Tu t'appelles comment?

The response would be:

Je m'appelle (your name).

Activités

A Walk around the classroom. Greet each of your classmates. Find out who each one is. Let each one know who you are.

B With a friend, walk up to a classmate. Pretending you don't know him or her, tell the classmate who your friend is. Then find out if he or she is a friend of the same person.

Culture

French Spelling

Many American students think spelling is a difficult subject. English words are not easy to spell because many different sounds are spelled or written the same way. French students also find spelling difficult. You will note that many French words sound the same but are spelled differently:

Nathalie est une *amie* de Jean-Luc.
Et David est un *ami* de Jean-Luc.

12 ◆ J*e suis de...*

Telling Where I Am From

—Tu es d'où, David?

—Moi, je suis de Dallas.

—Ah, tu es américain.

—Oui, je suis américain. Et toi, Nathalie, tu es d'où?

—Je suis de Lyon. Je suis française.

Note the difference in sound and spelling when describing a boy and a girl:

Je suis *américaine.*

Je suis *française.*

Nathalie est *française.*

Je suis *américain.*

Je suis *français.*

David est *américain.*

Activités

A   **Answer the following questions about yourself.**

1. Tu t'appelles comment?
2. Et tu es d'où?
3. Tu es de quelle nationalité?

B   **Draw a picture of a female friend or relative. Give her a French name. Then tell as much about her as you can.**

C   **Draw a picture of a male friend or relative. Give him a French name. Then tell as much about him as you can.**

D   **Work with a classmate. Find out where he or she is from and his or her nationality. Then give the same information about yourself.**

Récapitulons!

—Salut!

   —Salut!

—Tu es un ami de Jean-Luc, n'est-ce pas?

   —Oui, je suis David Sanders.

—Ça va, David?

   —Oui, ça va bien. Et toi?

—Pas mal.

   —Tu es Nathalie Gaudin, n'est-ce pas?

—Oui, je suis Nathalie.

   —Tu es d'où, Nathalie?

—Je suis de Lyon.

   —Ah, tu es française.

—Oui. Et toi, tu es américain, n'est-ce pas?

   —Oui, je suis de Dallas.

Activités

A Practice the conversation on page 134 with a classmate. Use as much expression as you can.

B Complete the following story about David and Nathalie.

David est de _____ au Texas. David est _____. _____ est de Lyon. Elle est _____. Nathalie est une _____ de Jean-Luc.

C Look at the photograph of Julie Carter. She is from Cleveland. Tell all about her.

D Look at this photograph of Patrick Benoît. He is from Rennes, France. Tell all about him.

*C*ulture

French-Speaking Cities

Montreal is a beautiful city in the Canadian province of Quebec. It was founded in 1642. Montreal, with some three million people, is the second largest French-speaking city in the world. The largest, of course, is Paris.

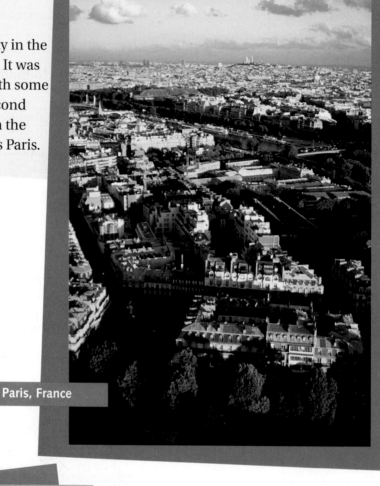

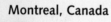
Paris, France

Montreal, Canada

French Online

For more information about Paris, Montreal, and other French-speaking cities, go to the Glencoe Web site: glencoe.com

13 ◆ J*e parle français*

—Tu parles anglais, David?

   —Oui, je parle anglais. Tu parles français, Nathalie?

—Oui, je parle français.

   —Tu parles anglais aussi?

—Oui, un petit peu.

As you can see, French words are often pronounced the same even though they are spelled differently:

—Tu *parles?*

   —Oui, je *parle.*

—Et Jean-Luc *parle* aussi?

   —Il *parle* français.

—Et Nathalie?

   —Elle *parle* français aussi.

Remember that you use *tu* to speak to a friend, *je* to speak about yourself, and *il* or *elle* to speak about someone else.

Activités

A Walk around the room and greet a classmate. Find out what language(s) he or she speaks. Then tell your classmate what language(s) you speak.

B Get a beach ball. One person throws the ball to another as he or she asks, *Tu parles français?* The person who catches the ball answers, *Je parle...*

C If you speak a language other than English at home, tell the class what language you speak.

Look at the French names of these languages. Since they are cognates, you can probably guess at their meaning:

italien	polonais
espagnol	arabe
portugais	grec
chinois	hébreu
japonais	swahili
vietnamien	

CENTRE POUR LA COMMUNICATION FRANCE JAPON

COURS PRATIQUES DE

JAP●NAIS

12, RUE DES PYRAMIDES 75001 PARIS • ☎ : 44 58 98 98 • M : PYRAMIDES

OKAPI

dans le journal d'actualité
EURO
INTERVIEW DE BRUNO MARTINI ET ERIC DI MECO

le monde s'ouvre aux 10-15 ans

GRAND DOSSIER

Le Japon
aujourd'hui

Did you know that Japanese is studied in France?

Culture

The French-Speaking World

Here are two friends from different areas of the world. They both have something very important in common. They both speak French.

Bonjour. Je m'appelle Ahmed.
Je suis d'Algiers en Algérie.
Je parle français et arabe.

Bonjour. Je m'appelle Mireille.
Je suis de Toulouse en France.
Je parle français.

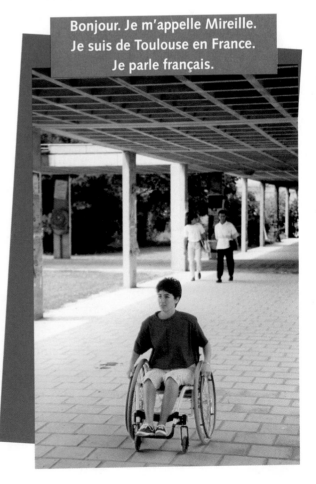

14 ◆ *J'aime...*

—Carole, tu aimes les maths?

　—Moi, oui. J'aime bien les maths.

—Et Henri, tu aimes les maths?

　—Pas du tout. Je n'aime pas les maths.

Note once again that French words are very often pronounced the same even though they are spelled differently:

—Tu *aimes* les maths?

　—Oui, j'*aime* les maths.

—Carole *aime* les maths aussi.

　—Mais Henri n'*aime* pas les maths.

Saying "No"

Here's how you say "no" to someone:

Non, je *ne* suis *pas* français.

Non, je *ne* parle *pas* espagnol.

Non, je *n'*aime *pas* les maths.

Activités

A **Work with a classmate. Find out what subjects each of you likes or dislikes. You can guess at the words you'll need to use since they are cognates.**

le français   l'histoire

l'anglais   l'art

les maths   la musique

les sciences   la gymnastique

B **Get a beach ball. One person throws the ball to another as he or she asks, *Tu aimes* _____? naming a particular subject. The person who catches the ball answers, *J'aime...* or *Je n'aime pas...***

Music class,
Montreal, Canada

C Tell a classmate about one of your classes—French, for example. Use the following questions as a guide.

1. Tu aimes le français?
2. Qui est le prof de français?
3. Le cours de français est intéressant?
4. Le cours de français est à quelle heure?
5. Tu parles français en classe?

D Read the following story about Paul and Nathalie.

Paul est américain. Il est de Dallas. Paul parle anglais. Et il parle français aussi. Il parle un peu. Il aime le français. Le cours de français est très intéressant. Mais Paul n'aime pas les maths. Il déteste les maths.

Nathalie n'est pas américaine. Elle est française. Elle est de Lyon. Nathalie parle français. Et elle parle anglais. Elle parle un petit peu. Elle aime l'anglais. Le cours d'anglais est très intéressant. Mais Nathalie n'aime pas la biologie. Elle déteste les sciences.

E Work with a classmate. One of you will ask the questions about Paul and the other will answer the questions. Then you'll switch parts for the questions about Nathalie.

Élève A

1. Paul est de quelle nationalité?
2. Il parle quelle langue?
3. Il aime le français?
4. Il déteste le français?

Élève B

1. Nathalie est de quelle nationalité?
2. Elle est d'où?
3. Elle parle quelle langue?
4. Elle aime l'anglais?
5. Elle n'aime pas quel cours?

Culture

School Schedule

In French schools, classes for all subjects do not meet every day. Some meet twice a week and others may meet four times a week. For this reason, French students take more courses each semester than American students do.

Lycée Janson,
Paris, France

Lycée Henri IV,
Paris, France

15 **M**a maison

Describing My House

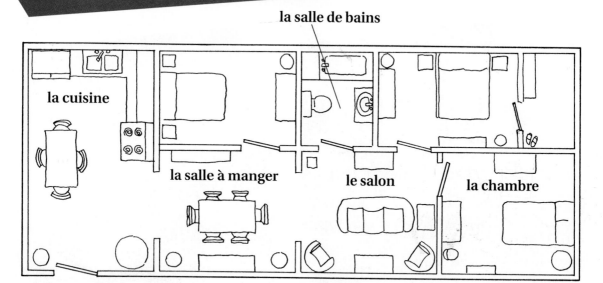

la salle de bains

la cuisine

la salle à manger

le salon

la chambre

l'appartement

Il y a means "there is" or "there are" in French:

Il y a un jardin autour de
la maison.

Il y a une voiture dans le garage.

Il y a dix pièces dans la maison.
C'est une grande maison.

le garage

la voiture

le jardin

la maison

une petite maison

Activités

A Draw a picture of your house. Write the title *Ma maison* at the top of your drawing. Then answer the following questions.

1. Ta maison est grande ou petite?
2. Il y a combien de pièces dans ta maison?
3. Il y a un jardin autour de la maison?

B Look at the photographs of the interior of a house in Strasbourg, France. Give the name in French for each room.

C Describe your dream house to a classmate. Say as much as you can about it in French.

Activités

A Look at the address book below and give the following information.

1. l'adresse de Madame Boileau
2. le numéro de téléphone de Madame Boileau

NUMÉRO DE TÉLÉPHONE/ADRESSE
NOM Marie Boileau
ADRESSE 3 rue de la Paix
75002 Paris
Numéro de téléphone
47.68.59.32

B Give the following information about yourself.

1. mon adresse
2. mon numéro de téléphone

POUR TÉLÉPHONER
CHOISISSEZ VOTRE HEURE

TELECARTE
50 UNITÉS

A French telephone card

16 · **M**a famille

Describing My Family

ma grand-mère   mon grand-père

mon oncle   ma tante

ma mère   mon père

ma cousine   mon cousin

mon frère   moi   ma sœur

Oncle Maurice est le frère de ma mère.
Et tante Geneviève est la sœur de ma mère.

Le fils de tante Geneviève est mon cousin.
Et la fille de tante Geneviève est ma cousine.

Activité

A Draw your family tree and identify your relatives in French.

Talking About My Family

—Tu as un frère?

  —Oui, j'ai un frère. (ou) Non, je n'ai pas de frère.

—Tu as combien de frères?

  —J'ai deux frères.

—Tu as une grande famille ou une petite famille?

  —J'ai une _____ famille. Il y a _____ personnes
  dans ma famille.

When you hear a question with *tu as* in French, you answer
with *j'ai. Tu as* is used to speak to a friend and *j'ai* is used to speak
about yourself.

tu as? → **j'ai**

To answer "yes" or "no" to a question, you say:

Tu as *un* frère?

Oui, j'ai *un* frère.

Non, je n'ai pas *de* frère.

Tu as *une* sœur?

Oui, j'ai *une* sœur.

Non, je n'ai pas *de* sœur.

Tu as *des* cousins?

Oui, j'ai *des* cousins.

Non, je n'ai pas *de* cousins.

Activités

A **Answer the following questions about your family.**

1. Tu as une grande famille ou une petite famille?
2. Tu as des frères?
3. Tu as combien de frères?
4. Tu as des sœurs?
5. Tu as combien de sœurs?
6. Et il y a combien de personnes dans ta famille?

B **Work with a classmate. Ask each other questions about your families in French.**

C **Who is it? Answer in French.**

1. la fille de mon père
2. le fils de mon père
3. le frère de ma mère
4. la sœur de mon père
5. la mère de mon père
6. la fille de mon oncle

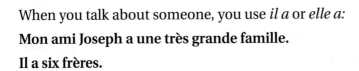

When you talk about someone, you use *il a* or *elle a*:

Mon ami Joseph a une très grande famille.

Il a six frères.

Activité

A Look at this photograph of *la famille Duvalier* from Toulouse, France. Describe the family in French.

Telling Age

To tell how old you or someone else is, you say:

J'ai douze ans.

Et mon frère a quinze ans.

To ask how old someone is, you say:

Et toi, tu as quel âge?

Do you know what this greeting card says in French?

Activités

A Ask each of your classmates his or her age. Tell each one your age.

B Give the ages of some of your friends and relatives.

Culture

The Family in French Culture

Just as in the United States, many French teenagers have step-parents and step-brothers or sisters. In French, however, there are no specific words to express "stepbrother" or "stepsister." In the case of parents, you could say *belle-mère* or *beau-père,* but these terms are confusing. They mean both "stepmother" or "stepfather" and "mother-in-law" or "father-in-law." You would, therefore, say *le mari de ma mère* or *la femme de mon père.*

There are expressions for "half brother" and "half sister." They are *demi-frère* and *demi-sœur.*

French-Moroccan family, Paris, France

17 ◆ Un bon ami

Talking About My Pet

des oiseaux

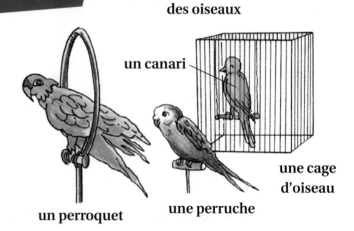

un canari

un chien

une cage
d'oiseau

un perroquet

une perruche

un chat

des poissons

un guppy   un poisson rouge

un hamster

une gerboise

un aquarium

Telling What I Like

—Tu aimes les animaux?

   —Moi, j'adore les animaux.

—Tu as un chien?

   —Non, je n'ai pas de chien. Mais
   j'ai un chat. J'adore mon petit
   chat. Il est adorable.

Activités

A **Answer the following personal questions in French.**

1. Tu aimes les animaux?

2. Tu as un chat ou un chien? Tu aimes ton chat ou ton chien?
   Il est adorable?

3. Tu as un oiseau? Tu as quel type d'oiseau? Tu as un canari,
   un perroquet?

4. Tu aimes les poissons? Tu as des poissons? Tu as un
   aquarium?

B **Ask a classmate all about his or her pet. Use the following
questions as a guide.**

1. Qu'est-ce que tu as? Tu as un chien? Un chat? Un oiseau?

2. Il a quel âge?

3. Il est adorable?

Telling What My Pet Does

Le chien aboie. Il saute.

Le chat miaule. Il saute aussi.

Le perroquet parle.

Le poisson nage
dans l'aquarium.

Le canari chante.

Culture

Animal Talk in French

Every language has its words for animal sounds. In English, a dog says "woof-woof" and a cat says "meow." What do the French animals say?

le chien: "ouah ouah"	le canard: "coin coin"
le chat: "miaou"	l'oiseau: "cuicui"
le mouton: "bê"	le cochon: "groin groin"

Compare these animal sounds with the animal sounds you know in English.

Pour leur assurer un bon départ.

Commencez ici.

Puppy Chow et Chow Chaton fournissent les vitamines, minéraux et éléments nutritifs supplémentaires si importants durant la première année de votre petit compagnon.

What do you think this French ad describes?

Activités

A Tell if the following animals or pets play.

1. le poisson rouge   4. le perroquet
2. le chien   5. le hamster
3. la gerboise   6. le chat

B Match the name of the animal with what it does.

1. un perroquet   a. il chante
2. un chat   b. il nage
3. un oiseau   c. il parle
4. un poisson   d. il saute

Culture

French Pets

There is no word in French that means "pet." This does not mean to say, however, that the French do not have pets. In fact, pets are more common in France than in any other European country. The French adore their pets. Cats and dogs are the most popular pets and the French take their dogs everywhere. It is not the least unusual in France to see *un chien* in a restaurant or supermarket.

18 ◆ **L**es sports

Talking About Sports

le base-ball

une équipe

le ballon

le volley(-ball)

un terrain
de foot(ball)

le foot(ball)

la balle

un court de tennis

le tennis

le joueur

la joueuse

le basket(-ball)

—Gilles, tu joues au foot?

—Oui, je joue au foot.

—Tu es dans l'équipe de ton école?

—Oui. Et c'est une très bonne équipe.

Activités

A Write up a list of the sports that you enjoy playing.

Je joue au...
J'aime...

B Get a beach ball. One student throws the ball to another. The one who throws the ball asks a question with *Tu joues.* The one who catches the ball answers, *Oui, je joue...* or *Non, je ne joue pas...*

C Answer the following personal questions.

1. Tu aimes les sports?

2. Tu préfères quel sport? Quel est ton sport favori?

3. Tu joues au _____?

4. Tu es dans l'équipe de ton école?

5. C'est une bonne équipe?

D **Give the following information about your favorite sport.**

1. Quel est ton sport favori?

2. C'est un sport d'équipe?

3. Il y a combien de joueurs dans l'équipe?

4. Tu joues au _____?

*C*ulture

Le Tour de France

The Tour de France is the most famous bicycle race in the world. It takes place in July. The course is changed every year, but there are always several *étapes* through the Pyrenees and the Alps. The finish line is always in Paris on the Champs-Élysées. In recent years, the course has gone through one or more neighboring countries, including Belgium, Germany, or Spain.

19 $\diamond$ **L**es vêtements

Clothing

une chemise

un pantalon

une casquette

une jupe

des chaussures

un tee-shirt

une blouse

un survêtement

un blouson

un short

des tennis

un (blue) jean

The word *on* is very useful in French. It can mean "we," "people," or "one."

On joue au tennis.

Et quand on joue au tennis on porte des tennis.

Activités

A In French, tell what you are wearing today.

Aujourd'hui je porte...

Department Store,
Paris, France

B Talk about the dress code in your school. Tell what you wear to class:

On porte _____ en classe.

And tell what you don't wear to class:

On ne porte pas de _____.

C Match the article of clothing with the color.

a. rouge

b. gris

c. jaune

d. marron

e. bleu

Culture

Clothing Today

Take a look at these photographs of French-speaking students your age. Note that they wear the same clothing that you and your friends do.

Chartres, France

Pointe-à-Pitre, Guadeloupe

Welcome to
Italian!

Italian is the language of the arias of the world's most beautiful operas—*Aida*, *Tosca*, and *Madama Butterfly*. Italian, like Spanish and French, is a Romance language derived from Latin. It is the language of Italy, the country where the original Latin was spoken. Italian is also the language of one section, or canton, of Switzerland.

When we think of Italian culture, the names of many famous artists and writers come to mind—Michelangelo, Dante, Raphael, and Leonardo da Vinci. Italy has given birth to so many writers, artists, philosophers, and musicians that it is often called the "cradle of Western civilization."

Italian is the mother tongue of many Americans of Italian origin. It is also spoken by many people of Italian descent in Argentina, Uruguay, and Chile.

Venice, Italy

REPUBBLICA DI SAN MARINO

Imperia, Italy

"Leaning Tower," Pisa, Italy

TEMPIETTO DI BRAMANTE
A. S. PIETRO IN MONTORIO

Dolomite Alps, northern Italy

Italian to English

As you study Italian, you will recognize many words of Italian origin. This is particularly true of the language of classical music:

alto	crescendo	solo
andante	libretto	soprano
aria	opera	staccato
basso	piano	

The Italian language also provides us with words for delicious foods and drinks:

cappuccino	pasta	ravioli
espresso	prosciutto	spaghetti
lasagna		

165

1 Ciao!

Greeting People

—Ciao, Giovanni!

—Ciao, Maria! Come stai?

—Bene, grazie, e tu?

—Non c'è male, grazie.

When speaking Italian, you must decide between formal and informal speech. The conversation above is between friends. If you were speaking to an adult you did not know well, you would say *Come sta?* rather than *Come stai?* You would also say *E Lei?* instead of *E tu?*

—Buon giorno, signora.

—Buon giorno, signorina. Come sta?

—Molto bene, grazie, e Lei?

—Molto bene, grazie.

Buon giorno and *buona sera* are more formal greetings than *ciao.* You would say *buon giorno* (A.M.) or *buona sera* (P.M.) when greeting adults, for example.

Buon giorno, signora.   **Buona sera, signorina.**

When you address a woman, the titles *signora* or *signorina* are almost always used in Italian. The last name of the person may be added, but it's not necessary. The title, *signore,* however, is seldom used when addressing a man. But if you know the man's name, you could say:

Buon giorno, signor Calabrese.

Attività

A Get up from your desk and walk around the classroom. Say *buon giorno* to each classmate you meet.

B Draw and cut out five stick figures. Give each one a name. They will represent your friends, family, and teachers. Greet each of your stick figures properly in Italian.

As you already know, you can ask *Come stai?* or *Come sta?* to find out how someone is feeling. There are several ways to express how you are feeling or how things are going for you. Some common expressions are:

Bene, grazie.	**Abbastanza bene.**
Molto bene.	**Non c'è male.**
Benissimo.	**Così così.**

Attività

A Work with a classmate. Make up a conversation in Italian. Greet each other and find out how things are going.

B Look at these photographs of people greeting each other in Verona, Italy. Do they do some of the things we do when they greet each other? Do they do some things that are different? Explain.

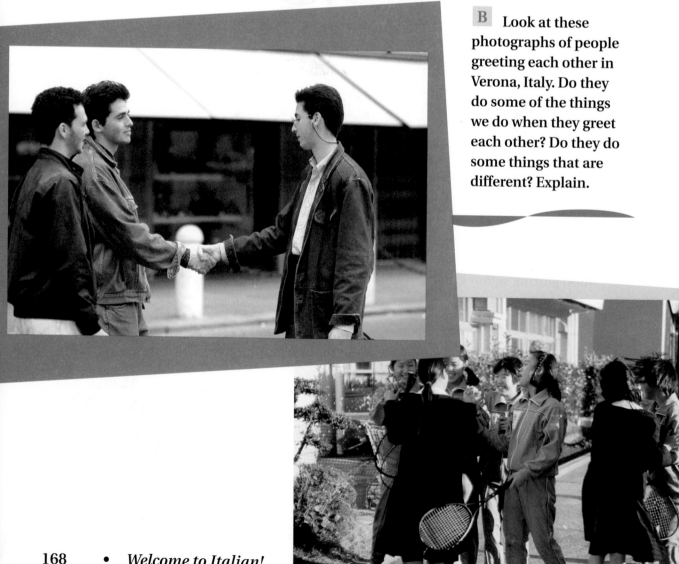

2 $\diamond$ *Arrivederci!*

Saying "Good-bye"

—Arrivederci, Carlo!
—Arrivederci, Teresa!

—Ciao, Marco!
—Ciao, Rosangela! A più
tardi.

The usual expression to use when saying "good-bye" to someone is:

Arrivederci.

You can also say arrivederLa when you want to be very formal.

If you plan to see the person again soon, you can say:

A più tardi.

A presto.

Ci vediamo.

If you plan to see the person the next day, you can say:

A domani.

The informal expression ciao can be used both to greet someone or to say "good-bye" to someone. It can mean "hi" or "bye." This popular Italian expression is used in other languages, too. You will hear it frequently in Spain, France, and Germany.

Attività

A Go over to a classmate. Say "so long" to him or her and then return to your seat.

B Work with a friend in class. Say "good-bye" to each other and let each other know that you'll be getting together again soon.

C Say "good-bye" to your teacher in Italian and then say "good-bye" to a friend. Don't forget to use a different expression with each person!

170 • *Welcome to Italian!*

Parliamo di più

—Buon giorno, Carlo.

   —Ciao, Franca. Come stai?

—Bene, grazie, e tu?

   —Non c'è male.

—Ciao, Carlo! A più tardi.

   —Arrivederci, Franca! A presto.

Attività

A   Work with a friend. Speak Italian together. Have fun saying as much as you can to one another!

B   Look at these photographs of people saying "good-bye" in an Italian section of San Francisco and in Bologna, Italy. Describe what the people are doing.

Bologna, Italy

San Francisco, California

2 · *Arrivederci!* • 171

Cultura

Common First Names

The following are some common names used for boys and girls in Italian.

Ragazzi

Antonio, Beppino, Carlo, Cesare, Dino, Franco, Gianni, Giorgio, Giuseppe, Luciano, Luigi, Maurizio, Michele, Paolo, Pietro, Riccardo, Sergio, Vincenzo

Ragazze

Anna, Clara, Claudia, Daniela, Domenica, Franca, Gigi, Giovanna, Giulia, Isabella, Luisa, Marcella, Maria, Marta, Patrizia, Pina, Rosangela, Teresa, Vittoria

Can you find the Italian names in these friendship ads below?

● CIAO, SONO UNA RA-GAZZA DI 15 ANNI, adoro lo sport, la musica e il cinema; vorrei corrispondere con ragazzi/e di ogni età. Scrive-temi, la risposta è assicurata! Vittoria Callegari, via Lussino 12, 21560 Stretti

● SONO UN RAGAZZO DI QUASI 15 ANNI. Amo ogni cosa che mi possa rallegrare e il giallo (anche i gelati!!). Scrivetemi e vi risponderò. Giulio Mantovani, via Cador-na 15/A, 30020 Roma

Milan, Italy

● SONO UNA RAGAZZA DI 16 ANNI, ammiratrice di Amedeo Minghi. Vorrei corrispondere con per-sone che amino la sua musica per scambiarci materiale e magari incon-trarci. Donatella Zanchetta, via Valdivisenza 10, 67793 Padova

Italian Online

For more information about Milan and other cities in Italy, go to the Glencoe Web site: glencoe.com

3 | *In classe*

Identifying Classroom Objects

To find out what something is, you ask:

Cos'è? (or) **Che cos'è?**

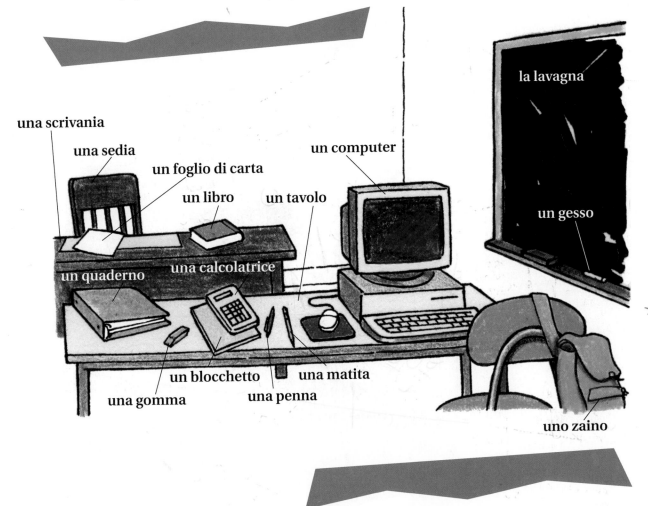

una scrivania

una sedia

un foglio di carta

un libro

un tavolo

un computer

la lavagna

un gesso

un quaderno

una calcolatrice

un blocchetto

una gomma

una penna

una matita

uno zaino

To ask for something in a polite way, you say:

Un foglio di carta, per favore.

Attività

A Ask a classmate for the following things in Italian. Don't forget to ask politely!

1.

2.

3.

4.

5.

6.

B Look at each picture and say in Italian what each person needs.

1.

2.

3.

$(x-2)(x^2+2x+4)$

4.

C Point to something in the classroom and ask a friend what it is.

*C*ultura

Schools in Italy

In Italy there are eight years of required schooling: five years of *scuola elementare* and three years of *scuola media.*

After finishing middle school, students decide whether or not to go on to four or five years of high school—four or five years of *scuola secondaria superiore.*

When they have completed five years of high school, students take a final exam—*l'esame di maturità.* If they pass the exam, they can enter the university of their choice.

Almost all schools in Italy are public and there is no tuition.

High school exam, Torino, Italy

4 ◆ Numeri

Counting in Italian

1	uno	20	venti	40	quaranta
2	due	21	ventuno	50	cinquanta
3	tre	22	ventidue	60	sessanta
4	quattro	23	ventitré	70	settanta
5	cinque	24	ventiquattro	80	ottanta
6	sei	25	venticinque	90	novanta
7	sette	26	ventisei		
8	otto	27	ventisette	100	cento
9	nove	28	ventotto	200	duecento
10	dieci	29	ventinove	300	trecento
				400	quattrocento
11	undici	30	trenta	500	cinquecento
12	dodici	31	trentuno	600	seicento
13	tredici	32	trentadue	700	settecento
14	quattordici	33	trentatré	800	ottocento
15	quindici	34	trentaquattro	900	novecento
16	sedici	35	trentacinque		
17	diciassette	36	trentasei	1.000	mille
18	diciotto	37	trentasette	2.000	duemila
19	diciannove	38	trentotto		
		39	trentanove		

Look at the way the numbers one and seven are written in Italian:

Attività

A Your teacher will write some numbers on the chalkboard. Then he or she will call out the number in Italian and ask a student to circle the correct number.

B Work with a classmate. One of you will count from 20 to 30. The other will count from 40 to 50.

C Have a contest with a friend. See who can count the fastest from 1 to 100 by tens.

D Have a contest with a friend. Count from 100 to 1000 by hundreds.

Finding Out the Price

To find out how much something costs, you ask:

—Quanto è la calcolatrice, signora?
—Quattro euro.
—Grazie, signora.

Attività

A Work with a classmate. One of you will be the customer and the other will be the clerk at a stationery store. Make up a conversation to buy the following things.

il quaderno

la calcolatrice

4€

5€

la gomma

la penna

1€

2€

1€

la matita

25€ lo zaino

Cultura

Money Systems

The Italian monetary unit is the euro.

Attività

A Give the amount of each Italian coin and bill pictured below.

1.

2.

3.

4.

5 **Prego**

Speaking Politely

—Buon giorno.
—Buon giorno. Un espresso, per favore.

(The waiter brings the order.)
—Grazie.
  —Prego.

(A little later.)
—Quanto è il espresso, per favore?
　—Due euro.

Another way to say "please" is:

Per piacere.

Attività

A With a friend, practice role-playing and reading the dialogue on pages 181–182 aloud.

B You are at a *caffè* in Venezia Lido, Italy. Order the following things. Ask a classmate to be the server.

1. un caffè

2. un tè

3. un espresso

4. un cappuccino

5. una limonata

6. un'aranciata

7. una cola

C You would like to order the following foods at an Italian restaurant. Be polite when you order them!

1.

una bistecca

2.

una pizza

3.

manicotti

4.

spaghetti alla bolognese

5.

lasagna

Cultura

Foods of the Italian World

Italian cuisine, *la cucina italiana,* is considered one of the best in the entire world. Italian or Italian-American cooking is very popular everywhere in the United States. When we think of Italian food, we think of pasta. Pasta is made by mixing flour and water or flour and eggs in different proportions. You can add a variety of delicious sauces to the pasta.

Pasta comes in a wide range of shapes, sizes, thickness, and textures. All have different names. How many of these pastas do you know?

capellini	**ravioli**
farfalle	**spaghetti**
lasagne	**tortellini**
linguine	**vermicelli** (or) **spaghettini**
maccheroni	**ziti**
penne	

6 ◆ Che ora è?

Telling Time

To find out the time, you ask:

Che ora è? (or) **Che ore sono?**

To tell the time, you say:

È l'una.　　**Sono le due.**　　**Sono le tre.**　　**Sono le quattro.**

Sono le cinque.　　**Sono le sei.**　　**Sono le sette.**　　**Sono le otto.**

Sono le nove.　　**Sono le dieci.**　　**Sono le undici.**　　**Sono le dodici.**

È l'una
e cinque.

Sono le due
e dieci.

Sono le cinque
e quaranta.

Sono le sei e un
quarto. Sono le
sei e quindici.

Sono le sette
e mezzo. Sono le
sette e trenta.

Attività

A Give the following times in Italian.

B Walk up to a classmate and ask for the time. Your classmate will answer you.

Telling At What Time

To find out at what time something takes place, you ask:
A che hora è la lezione?

To tell at what time something takes place, you answer:
La lezione è alle nove e trenta.

Attività

A Tell at what time you have the following classes. Note that these words are cognates. They are very similar in both Italian and English.

1. la lezione di matematica
2. la lezione di storia
3. la lezione d'educazione fisica
4. la lezione di biologia
5. la lezione d'italiano
6. la lezione d'inglese

B Draw pictures of some of your daily activities such as getting up in the morning, eating breakfast, walking or riding the bus to school, going to after-school sports, eating dinner, going to bed, etc. Then compare your pictures with those of a classmate. Both of you will tell when you do these activities. Keep track of how many activities you both do at the same time.

Cultura

Lunch Customs

In Italy, many people still go home for lunch. Businesses close at 1:00 *(all'una)* in the afternoon and open again between 4:30 and 5:00 *(alle quattro e mezzo o alle cinque)*. Because of the traffic problems in the large cities, however, many people now eat where they work or go to a nearby *caffè*, *trattoria*, or *paninoteca*.

PINOCCHIO PIZZERIA

PINOCCHIO

PIZZERIA - Specialita' carne e pesce alla brace
Chiuso il venerdi'

MILANO: v. V. Foppa, 16
(ang. v. California) ☎ (02) 481 47 73

Bakery,
Naples, Italy

Café near the Pantheon,
Rome, Italy

7 | **I** *giorni della settimana*

Telling the Days of the Week

Finding Out and Giving the Day

—Che giorno è oggi?
  —È lunedì.
    (or) Oggi è lunedì.

—Che giorno è domani?
  —È martedì.
    (or) Domani è martedì.

Attività

A Answer the following questions in Italian.

1. Che giorno è oggi?
2. E domani? Che giorno è?
3. Quali sono i giorni del week-end, del fine settimana?

*C*ultura

Italian-American Festivals

There are wonderful Italian street fairs held in many cities of the United States where there is a large Italian-American population. Many of these fairs are organized by the local Italian parish church. Quite often the *festa* is in honor of the patron saint of the parish.

A famous *festa italiana* is the Feast of San Gennaro, celebrated each summer in Little Italy, a section of New York City.

San Gennaro Festival,
New York City

S. GENNARO

St. Anthony's Festival,
Boston

8 — Mesi e stagioni

Telling the Months

GENNAIO	FEBBRAIO	MARZO	APRILE	MAGGIO	GIUGNO
1 2 3 4 5 6	1 2 3	1 2	1 2 3 4 5 6	1 2 3 4	1
7 8 9 10 11 12 13	4 5 6 7 8 9 10	3 4 5 6 7 8 9	7 8 9 10 11 12 13	5 6 7 8 9 10 11	2 3 4 5 6 7 8
14 15 16 17 18 19 20	11 12 13 14 15 16 17	10 11 12 13 14 15 16	14 15 16 17 18 19 20	12 13 14 15 16 17 18	9 10 11 12 13 14 15
21 22 23 24 25 26 27	18 19 20 21 22 23 24	17 18 19 20 21 22 23	21 22 23 24 25 26 27	19 20 21 22 23 24 25	16 17 18 19 20 21 22
28 29 30 31	25 26 27 28 29	24 25 26 27 28 29 30	28 29 30	26 27 28 29 30 31	23 30 24 25 26 27 28 29

LUGLIO	AGOSTO	SETTEMBRE	OTTOBRE	NOVEMBRE	DICEMBRE
1 2 3 4 5 6	1 2 3	1 2 3 4 5 6 7	1 2 3 4 5	1 2	1 2 3 4 5 6 7
7 8 9 10 11 12 13	4 5 6 7 8 9 10	8 9 10 11 12 13 14	6 7 8 9 10 11 12	3 4 5 6 7 8 9	8 9 10 11 12 13 14
14 15 16 17 18 19 20	11 12 13 14 15 16 17	15 16 17 18 19 20 21	13 14 15 16 17 18 19	10 11 12 13 14 15 16	15 16 17 18 19 20 21
21 22 23 24 25 26 27	18 19 20 21 22 23 24	22 23 24 25 26 27 28	20 21 22 23 24 25 26	17 18 19 20 21 22 23	22 23 24 25 26 27 28
28 29 30 31	25 26 27 28 29 30 31	29 30	27 28 29 30 31	24 25 26 27 28 29 30	29 30 31

Telling the Seasons

la primavera

l'estate

l'autunno

l'inverno

Finding Out and Giving the Date

—Qual è la data di oggi?

—Oggi è il primo aprile.

Primo is used for the first of the month. For other days, you use *due, tre, quattro,* etc.: *il due maggio.*

Attività

A Each of you will stand up in class and give the date of your birthday in Italian. Listen and keep a record of how many of you were born in the same month.

B Based on the information from *Attività A,* tell in Italian in which months most of the students in the class were born. Tell in what month the fewest were born.

C Work in groups of two or three. Each group is responsible for drawing a calendar for one month of the year. Include the dates of classmates' birthdays.

D In which season of the year is . . . ?

1. dicembre
2. maggio
3. aprile
4. luglio

Look at the ad below. Tell when each Italian film is shown.

TEATRO ARGENTINA

DAL 1 ALL'8 OTTOBRE

Nostra Signora srl
MACBETH HORROR SUITE
di Carmelo Bene
da William Shakespeare

PROGETTO ACQUARIO

quartiere Esquilino

DAL 2 AL 20 OTTOBRE

Compagnia di Giorgio Barberio Corsetti
LA NASCITA DELLA TRAGEDIA
testo e regia di Giorgio Barberio Corsetti

TEATRO VITTORIA

DAL 9 AL 20 OTTOBRE

Teatro Nero Ta Fantastika di Praga
LA PARABOLA DI DON CHISCIOTTE
testo e regia di Petr Kratochvil

ROMA FILM FESTIVAL

Al Palazzo delle Esposizioni e nelle sale
cinematografiche.
Selezione di pellicole italiane e straniere e
retrospettiva Rossellini.

DALL'11 AL 18 NOVEMBRE

9 ◆ **I**l tempo

Describing the Weather

—Che tempo fa oggi?
   —Fa bello. Fa bel tempo.
      C'è sole.

—Fa cattivo tempo.
   Fa brutto.
   Piove.

Tira vento.

Nevica.

Fa caldo. Non fa fresco.

Fa freddo.

Attività

A Tell in Italian what the weather is like today.

B Work in groups of four. Write in Italian the name of each season on a separate sheet of paper. Put the papers in a pile. Each of you will pull one sheet from the pile. Then describe the weather of the season written on the sheet.

C Draw a picture of your favorite type of weather. Then describe your picture to the class in Italian.

Cultura

Seasons in Italy

Italy enjoys a wonderful climate. In the winter, skiers flock to ski resorts such as Cortina d'Ampezzo. In summer, sun-lovers enjoy the beaches of the Mediterranean or the Adriatic such as Portofino or Venezia Lido.

Can you tell what the weather is like today in northern Italy and in southern Italy from this weather map below? How about tomorrow's weather?

Portofino, Italy

Ski resort,
Cervinia, Italy

10 ◆ *Sono...*

—Buon giorno. Tu sei un amico di Gianni Rossi, non è vero?

—Sì, sono Mark Thomson. E tu sei Luciana, vero?

—Sì, sono Luciana. Luciana Carlucci. Sei americano, Mark?

—Sì, sono americano. Sono di Nuova York.

When you hear a question with *sei* in Italian, you answer with *sono*. *Sei* is used to speak to a friend *(tu)* and *sono* is used to speak about yourself *(io)*.

Sei? → **sono**

When you describe a boy in Italian, you use *-o*. When you describe a girl, you use *-a*.

Ricardo non è *italiano*.   Giulia non è *americana*.

Ricardo è *americano*.   Giulia è *italiana*.

Ricardo è *un amico* di Gianni. Giulia è *un'amica* di Luigi.

Attività

A Work with a classmate. Practice reading aloud the dialogue on page 198. Use as much expression as possible!

B Walk up to a classmate. Pretend that you think that you remember his or her name, but you aren't sure. Then find out if he or she is a friend of someone you know.

C Answer the following questions about yourself.

1. Sei americano(a)?
2. Di dove sei?
3. Sei un amico (un'amica) di Marcello Scotti?

D Draw a picture of a male friend or relative. Give him an Italian name. Then tell as much about him as you can.

E Draw a picture of a female friend or relative. Give her an Italian name. Then tell as much about her as you can.

Parliamo di più

—Ciao!

    —Ciao!

—Sei un amico di
Franco Marotto,
non è vero?

    —Sì, sono un amico
di Franco. Sono
Mark Thomson.

—Come stai, Mark?

    —Molto bene,
grazie, e tu?

—Non c'è male.

    —Sei Luciana, no?

—Sì, sono Luciana.

    —Sei di Roma, Luciana?

—No, io sono di Milano. Ma tu sei americano, non è vero?

    —Sì, sono di Nuova York.

—Ciao, Mark. A presto.

    —Arrivederci, Luciana. Ci vediamo.

Attività

A Work with a classmate. Practice the above conversation
together with a classmate. One will read the part of Mark and the
other will read the part of Luciana. Use as much expression as
you can.

B Complete the following story about Mark and Luciana.

Mark è di _____. Mark è _____, non è italiano. Mark è un _____
di Franco. Anche Luciana è un'amica di _____. Luciana non è
americana. È _____. Non è di Roma. È _____ Milano.

C Work with a classmate. Find out where he or she is from
and his or her nationality. Then give the same information
about yourself.

D Look at the photograph of Paula Wright. She is from Houston. Tell all about her in Italian.

E Look at this photograph of Bianca Pretti. She is from Venezia. Tell all about her in Italian.

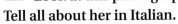

11 ◆ **P**_arlo italiano_

Telling What I Speak and Study

—Parli inglese, David?

   —Sì, parlo inglese.

—Parli anche l'italiano?

   —Sì, parlo un po', non molto.

—Studi l'italiano a scuola?

   —Sì, la lezione d'italiano è molto interessante.

When you hear a question with *parli* or *studi,* you answer with *parlo* or *studio. Parli* and *studi* are used when speaking to a friend *(tu)* and *parlo* and *studio* are used when speaking about yourself *(io).*

    Parli? → **parlo**   **Studi?** → **studio**

Look at the Italian names of these languages. You can probably guess the meaning of each as all of these words are cognates.

italiano	russo
francese	polacco
portoghese	arabo
cinese	greco
giapponese	latino

What languages are taught at this school in Miami?

PADOVAN LANGUAGE INSTITUTE

YOUR PASSPORT TO FLUENCY

CORSI DI:
- SPAGNOLO
- FRANCESE
- PORTOGHESE
- ITALIANO
- RUSSO
- TEDESCO

INGLESE DA LIVELLO 0 A LIVELLI AVANZATI
Preparazione al TOFEL
Tutti i livelli. Lezioni private o in gruppo.

Impara di più, in meno tempo con il Metodo Padovan!

CHIAMA OGGI STESSO!

(305) 375-0315

(dietro la chiesa)

Attività

A Walk around the room and greet a classmate. Find out what language(s) he or she speaks. Then tell your classmate what language(s) you speak.

B Get a beach ball. One person throws the ball to another and asks, *Parli italiano?* The person who catches the ball answers, *Sì, parlo...* or *No, non parlo...*

C If you speak a language other than English at home, tell the class what language you speak.

D Answer the following questions.

1. Studi la matematica? È facile o difficile la lezione di matematica?

2. Studi l'italiano a scuola? È facile o difficile la lezione d'italiano?

CUCINA GIAPPONESE
ROKKO
Domenica Riposo
00187 ROMA
Via Rasella, 138 .... ☎ (06) 4 88 12 14

Ristorante Cinese
RU YI
L'ATMOSFERA CINESE IN UN AMBIENTE ELEGANTE
ARIA CONDIZIONATA
ROMA Via Valadier, 14 (in Prati)
☎ (06) 3 21 58 04

Welcome to
LATIN!

Latin is the mother tongue of all the Romance languages. The original home of Latin was Latium, a small district on the western coast of Italy. The chief city of Latium was Rome.

The Romans were often threatened by warlike neighbors. Unwilling to accept defeat, they sent out legions to conquer their enemies. By the middle of the third century B.C., the Romans had conquered all of Italy. Their legions continued beyond the Mediterranean Sea and the Alps. Rome soon became the capital of a tremendous empire and the center of a great civilization.

The Latin language spoken by the Roman armies was also the language of some of the western world's greatest writers and orators. Latin was the language of Vergil, Cicero, Catullus, Ovid, and Pliny. Even after the fall of the Roman Empire, Latin continued to be the language of a large part of Europe. It finally evolved into the modern Romance languages: French, Italian, Portuguese, Rumanian, and Spanish.

Roman aqueduct,
Nîmes, France

Colosseum, Rome, Italy

Roman theater,
Aphrodisia, Turkey

Appian Way,
Rome, Italy

Latin to English

Although English is not a Romance language, some 50% of all English words come from Latin. As you study Latin, you will learn Latin derivatives. Latin derivatives are words used in English that have Latin origins. Some examples are:

audīre (to hear) audio, audible, audience, audition
fortūna (fortune) fortunate, misfortune
grātia (favor, thanks) grace, gracious
liberāre (to free) liberal, liberator
medicus (doctor) medical, medicine

1 $\mathcal{S}$alvē et Valē

Greeting People

—Salvē.
  —Salvē.
—Quis es?
  —Sum Marcus.
—Et ego sum Anna.
  —Valē, Anna.
—Valē.

When you hear a question with *es* in Latin, you answer with *sum*. *Es* is used to speak to one person and *sum* is used to speak about yourself.

es? → **sum**

For emphasis, you can add *ego* with *sum*, but it isn't generally needed:

Ego sum Rōmāna.

Verba Latīna

The word "egoist" comes from the Latin word *ego*. What is an egoist, and what does it mean to have a big ego?

I...I...I....
..now let's talk about me for awhile..

Egoist

Agenda

A Get up from your desk and walk around the classroom. Say *Salvē* to each of your classmates and then say *Valē*.

B Get a beach ball. One person throws the ball as he or she asks *Quis es?* The one who catches the ball answers *Sum...*

Cultūra

Common First Names

Here are some Latin first names that were popular in the days of the Romans.

Puerī

Aemilius, Augustus, Claudius, Cornēlius, Davus, Fabius, Gāius, Horātius, Lūcius, Marcus, Maximus, Paulus, Publius, Quintus, Sextus, Tullus

Puellae

Aelēna, Aemilia, Anna, Aurēlia, Caecilia, Clāra, Claudia, Cornēlia, Fabia, Flavia, Glōria, Jūlia, Lāvīnia, Messalina, Sophia, Tullia

Here is a mosaic of a Roman man and two Roman women. A mosaic was a popular form of art in Roman times. It was made of colored pieces of stone or glass. This mosaic shows the Roman poet Vergil holding a papyrus roll. The two women on either side are Muses, who were goddesses of the arts.

The man—*vir Rōmānus*—is wearing the typical Roman clothing for an adult male—a *toga* over a tunic. The women—*fēminae Rōmānae*—are wearing the typical Roman clothing for an adult female—a *stola* over a tunic.

2 ◆ Numerī

Counting in Latin

1	ūnus	6	sex	11	ūndecim
2	duo	7	septem	12	duodecim
3	trēs	8	octō		
4	quattuor	9	novem	20	vīgintī
5	quinque	10	decem	100	centum
				1000	mille

Duo et trēs sunt quinque.

Quattuor et octo et sex et duo sunt vīgintī.

Agenda

A Count from one to ten in Latin.

B Make up some simple addition problems and ask a classmate for the answers.

Cultūra

Writing Numbers in Latin

The number system we use today is the Arabic system (1, 2, 3, etc.). The Romans used the Roman system shown below.

I	IV
II	V
III	

The Romans used only a limited number of letters to express numerals:

I	1	C	100
V	5	D	500
X	10	M	1000
L	50		

They combined or put letters together to form other numerals:

II	2	XI	11
IV	4	CLXIV	164

Arch of Titus, Rome, Italy

Roman numerals are still frequently used on monuments and buildings. They also are used for decorative purposes. What is the Arabic numeral for the Roman numeral on this house?

Agenda

A Give the Arabic numerals for each of the following Roman numerals.

1. II
2. IX
3. VI
4. XL

5. LX
6. XXV
7. XXVI
8. DL

B Try to think of at least two places where you would normally see Roman numerals used today.

Verba Latīna

Latin numbers provide us with many words in English. Let's take a look at a few of them. Tell what each of the following words means and then give the Latin numeral from which it is derived:

centennial	dual	quintuplets	unison
centipede	duet	trio	unite
century	millionaire	tripod	
decimal	octave	triple	

Ball III, Strike II

Look at the numbers below in three Romance languages. Which do you think are the most similiar to the original Latin?

Latīna	español	italiano	français
ūnus	uno	uno	un
duo	dos	due	deux
trēs	tres	tre	trois
quattuor	cuatro	quattro	quatre
quinque	cinco	cinque	cinq
sex	seis	sei	six
septem	siete	sette	sept
octō	ocho	otto	huit
novem	nueve	nove	neuf
decem	diez	dieci	dix
ūndecim	once	undici	onze

3 ◆ **P***aulus et Clāra*

Paulus est amīcus bonus.

Et Paulus est discipulus bonus.

Clāra est amīca bona.

Clāra est discipula bona quoque.

Vīlla est pulchra.

Sed vīlla est parva.

Vīlla nōn est magna.

Casa est parva quoque.

Casa nōn est magna.

Sed casa pulchra est.

To form a question in Latin, you add *-ne* to the first word in the sentence:

Estne Paulus discipulus Rōmānus?

Estne Clāra amīca bona?

Paulusne est discipulus Rōmānus?

To answer "yes" to a question, you can say:

Sic.

Ita vērō.

To answer "no" to a question, you can say:

Minimē.

Agenda

A   Answer the following questions in Latin.

1. Estne Paulus amīcus bonus?
2. Quis est amīcus bonus?
3. Et quis est amīca bona?
4. Quis est discipulus bonus?
5. Quis est discipula bona?
6. Estne vīlla pulchra?
7. Estne vīlla parva?
8. Estne casa magna?

B   Work in pairs. Ask each other questions about Paulus. Then ask each other questions about Clāra.

C   Work in groups of four. Point to someone in your group as you ask a question with *quis.* Call on someone else from the group to answer. The person who answers must use the name of the person you pointed to.

D   Work with a classmate. Make up a conversation using the following as a guide.

—Esne _____?

—Sic, ego sum _____.

—Esne discipulus/discipula?

—Ita vērō. Sum _____.

—Esne discipulus Americanus/discipula Americana?

—Sic, sum _____.

Cultūra

Houses in the Roman World

There are several words in Latin that mean "house." *Vīlla* is the word for country house. Many wealthy Romans had a house in the country. To escape Rome's bustling activities and noisy streets, they would go to their country house or *vīlla*, particularly in the summer. The J. Paul Getty Museum in California (below) is a modern reconstruction of a Roman *vīlla*.

In the city, people of the working and middle classes lived in *īnsulae,* or apartment buildings. Each *īnsula* was several stories high and had a number of individual apartments and shared cooking areas. On the following page there is a photograph of a model reconstruction of a five-story *īnsula* at Ostia, near Rome.

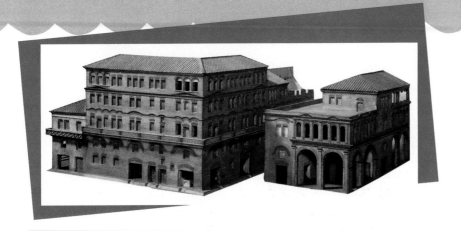

A *domus* was a self-contained house in the city. Only the nobles and very wealthy Romans had a *domus* in the city. Below is a photograph of an artist's reconstruction of a *domus*. It is based on archaeological remains in Pompeii, Italy.

Latin Online

For more information about Roman life, go to the Glencoe Web site: glencoe.com

INTERIOR OF A ROMAN HOUSE

A *casa* was a simple cottage for a fisherman or sailor on the Mediterranean coast. Very few examples exist today of these simple cottages. Can you guess why?

Verba Latīna

Find the Latin words that come from the following English words.

amicable	magnificent
castle	magnitude
disciple	pulchritude
domicile	villa

Verba Latīna

Looking at the following sentences. Which language seems closest to Latin?

Latin: *Paulus est amīcus bonus.*

French: *Paul est un bon ami.*

Spanish: *Pablo es un amigo bueno.* (or) *Pablo es un buen amigo.*

Italian: *Paolo è un amico buono.* (or) *Paolo è un buon amico.*

"Good," isn't it?

4 ◆ A*mīcī et Discipulī*

Talking About People

Paulus et Cornēlius
sunt amīcī.

Paulus et Cornēlius
sunt discipulī.

Paulus et Cornēlius
amīcī bonī sunt.

Puerī discipulī bonī
sunt.

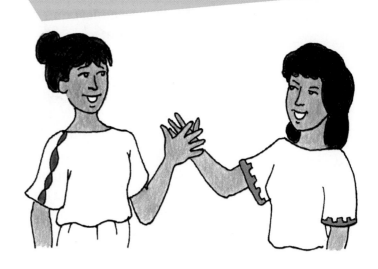

Jūlia et Claudia sunt amīcae.

Puellae sunt amīcae bonae.

Et Jūlia et Claudia sunt
discipulae bonae.

When you speak or write about more than one person, you must use the plural form. Here's how to form the plural in Latin:

Singular	*Plural*	*Singular*	*Plural*
amīcus	amīcī	amīca	amīcae
discipulus	discipulī	casa	casae

Verba Latīna

Read the following English sentences. Can you tell where the forms "alumnus/alumni" and "alumna/alumnae" come from?

John is an alumnus of Brown University.

Many of his friends are alumni of Brown University.

Erica is an alumna of UCLA.

Many of her friends are alumnae of UCLA.

Can you find the Latin word in this Harvard University seal? What does it mean in English?

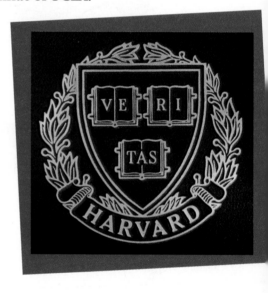

Agenda

A Answer the following questions in Latin.

1. Quī sunt amīcī?
2. Suntne amīcī bonī?
3. Quae sunt amīcae?
4. Suntne amīcae bonae?
5. Quī sunt discipulī bonī?
6. Quae sunt discipulae bonae?

B Answer the following questions in Latin.

1. Quis est discipulus bonus?
2. Quī sunt discipulī bonī?
3. Quis est discipula bona?
4. Quae sunt discipulae bonae?
5. Quis est Rōmānus?
6. Quae sunt Rōmānae?

C Here is a portrait of Flavius. Tell as much as you can about him in Latin.

D Here is a portrait of Flavius and Marcus. Tell as much as you can about them in Latin.

E Here is a portrait of Aemilia. Tell as much as you can about her in Latin.

F Here is a portrait of Aemilia and Claudia. Tell as much as you can about them in Latin.

G Read the following story and then complete the sentences. Note that many of the words are cognates, which means that they are almost the same in Latin and English.

Italia est patria pulchra. Italia in Europā est. Italia nōn est īnsula. Italia est paenīnsula magna.

Hispānia quoque paenīnsula est. Hispānia et Italia sunt paenīnsulae. Hispānia et Italia nōn sunt īnsulae. Hispānia et Italia sunt patriae pulchrae in Europā.

Britannia et Corsica et Sardinia īnsulae sunt. Nōn sunt paenīnsulae. Britannia magna īnsula est. Corsica et Sardinia parvae īnsulae sunt.

1. Italia est _____.
2. Italia et Hispānia sunt _____.
3. Sicilia est īnsula. Sicilia non est _____.
4. Sicilia et Corsica sunt _____.
5. Italia non est patria parva. Italia patria _____ est.
6. Italia et Hispānia sunt _____ magnae.
7. Et Sicilia et Corsica sunt _____ parvae.
8. Britannia est īnsula _____.

Verba Latīna

1. Read the story in *Agenda G* again. As you do, make a list of cognates you find.
2. Tell what Latin word these English words come from:

Hispanic   **patriotic**

insular   **peninsular**

Then give a definition of each English word.

Cultūra

Schooling in Roman Times

Students wrote on a wooden tablet called a *tabula*. It was covered with a thin layer of wax. Students scratched their letters on the wax surface with a thin stick of metal, bone, or ivory called a *stilus*. The Roman girl in this painting is holding a *tabula* and a *stilus*.

Roman students were usually escorted to school by a slave who looked after them. This slave was called a *paedagogus*. Another slave, the *capsarius,* carried their books and writing materials. The teacher or *magister* is to the right in this stone relief.

Roman boys and girls started school at about the age of seven. Only children of the middle and professional classes attended school. The very rich were tutored at home. Here, in this painting, a Roman matron teaches her daughter to read.

5 △ Amīcus amīcam videt

Word Order

Paulus Minervam videt.

Et Minerva Paulum videt.

Paulus Minervam amat.

Minerva Paulum amat.

Minerva bonum amīcum
Paulum amat.

Paulus bonam amīcam
Minervam amat.

Paulus epistulas scrībit.

Minerva epistulas legit.

In English, word order is very important. The position of the word in the sentence tells who does the action and who receives the action:

Paul sees Minerva.

The word before the verb "sees" does the action and the word that follows the verb "sees" receives the action. If you reverse them, it changes the meaning completely:

Minerva sees Paul.

In Latin, word order is not important. Latin uses endings to tell who does or receives the action:

Paulus videt Minervam.

Paulus Minervam videt.

Minervam videt Paulus.

Minerva videt Paulum.

Minerva Paulum videt.

Paulum videt Minerva.

Regardless of the word order, the message is clear because the endings tell who does or receives the action.

Doer	*Receiver*
Paulus	**Paulum**
discipulus	**discipulum**
Minerva	**Minervam**
puella	**puellam**

Verba Latīna

Explain the meaning of the following English words:

epistle	**scribe**
legible	**video**

What Latin word does each one come from?

Agenda

A **Answer the following questions in Latin.**

1. Quis videt Minervam?
2. Quem videt Paulus?
3. Quis videt Paulum?
4. Quem videt Minerva?
5. Quem amat Paulus?
6. Quis amat Paulum?
7. Quis scrībit epistulas?
8. Quis legit epistulas?

B **Read the following story about Cornēlius and Anna.**

Cornēlius et Anna in Italiā habitant. Italiā est patria pulchra. Cornēlius et Anna suam patriam amant. Quem amant Cornēlius et Anna?

C **Read the story once again. Then answer the question in the story.**

D **Here is a map of Italy and Sicily at the time of the Roman Empire. Working in pairs, say as much as you can in Latin about the map. You can also ask each other where a place is using** *Ubi est...*

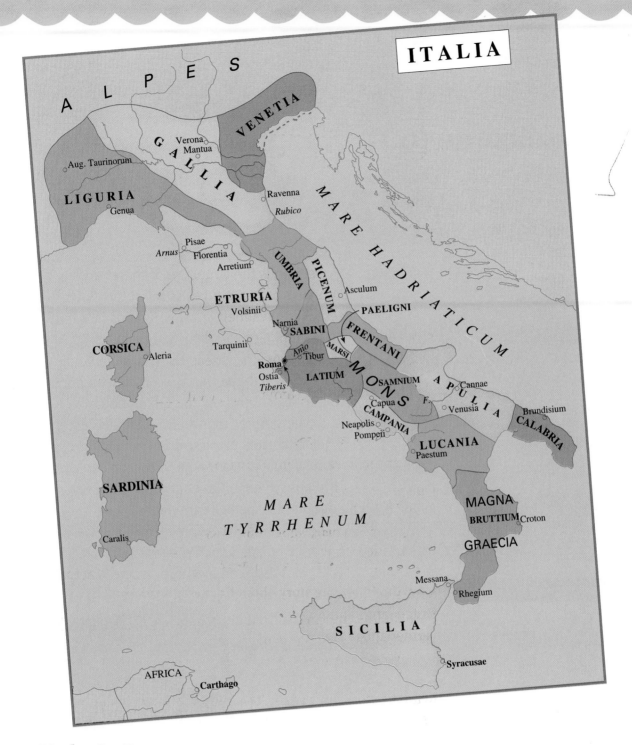

Verba Latīna

In the reading selection in *Agenda B,* you came across the
Latin word *habitant.* Guess at its meaning from the context of the
sentence. The following English words are derived from *habitant:*
inhabitant, habitation, to habitate. Do you know what these words
mean? If not, look them up in a dictionary.

Welcome to
GERMAN!

German is the language of these famous composers of beautiful classical music: Bach, Beethoven, Wagner, Strauss, Brahms, Mozart, and Haydn. German is the language of Germany, Austria, and most of Switzerland. It is also the language of two European principalities: Liechtenstein and Luxembourg.

Many Americans are of German descent. Their ancestors came to this country for economic, political, or religious reasons. In areas of Pennsylvania, Ohio, and Indiana, many people still speak Pennsylvania Dutch. The word "Dutch" comes from the German word *Deutsch* which means "German." The "Dutch" spoken by these people is actually a form of German, not the Dutch language spoken in the Netherlands.

Heidelberg Castle, Germany

Neuschwanstein Castle, Germany

Munich, Germany

Rhine River,
Germany

German to English

When you study German, you will come across many words
that you will recognize immediately. You will know what they
mean because we use them in English. Here are a few examples:

diesel   kindergarten   wienerschnitzel
dachshund   sauerkraut   wurst
frankfurter   strudel

1 Begrüßung

Greeting People

—Tag, Hans.

    —Tag, Eva. Wie geht's?

—Gut, danke. Und dir?

    —Nicht schlecht, danke.

Guten Tag is a more formal greeting than *Tag*. You would say *Guten Tag* when greeting adults, for example. You would also use the person's title and name:

Guten Tag, Herr Braun.

Guten Tag, Frau Wagner.

Guten Tag, Fräulein Schmitt.

Aktivitäten

A Get up from your desk and walk around the classroom. Say *Guten Tag* to each classmate you meet.

B Work with a classmate. Make up a conversation in German. Greet each other and find out how things are going.

When speaking German, you must decide between formal and informal speech. The conversation on page 230 is between friends. If you were speaking to an adult whom you did not know well, you would say *Wie geht es Ihnen?* rather than *Wie geht's?* You would also say *Und Ihnen?* instead of *Und dir?*

Formal	*Informal*
Wie geht es Ihnen?	**Wie geht's?**
Sehr gut. Und Ihnen?	**Sehr gut. Und dir?**

—Guten Tag, Frau Müller. Wie geht es Ihnen?

—(Es geht mir) sehr gut, danke. Und Ihnen?

—Sehr gut, danke.

Note that the most common answer to the formal *Wie geht es Ihnen?* is:

Es geht mir sehr gut, danke.

There are several different responses to the informal *Wie geht's?* They are:

Es geht.   **Ganz gut.**   **Nicht schlecht.**

Aktivitäten

A   Draw and cut out five stick figures. Give each one a name. They will represent your friends, family, and teachers. Greet each of your stick figures properly in German.

B   Work with a classmate. Make up a conversation in German. Greet each other and find out how things are going.

C   Look at these photographs below of German-speaking people greeting each other. Do they do some of the things we do when they greet each other? Do they do some things that are different? Explain.

Kultur

Germantown, USA

In many U.S. cities that have a large population of German descent, there is a section of the city called Germantown. In the Germantown section, you will find German delicatessens, butcher shops, and pastry shops. There will often be a good German restaurant.

German restaurant, San Francisco

German bakery, Chicago

◆2 **V**erabschieden

—Auf Wiedersehen, Ingrid.
—Auf Wiedersehen,
Dieter.

—Tschüs!
—Tschüs!

The usual expression to use when saying "good-bye" to someone is:

Auf Wiedersehen.

If you plan to see the person again soon, you can say:

Bis später.　　　　　　　　**Bis nachher.**

If you plan to see the person again very soon, you can say:

Bis bald.　　　　　　　　**Bis gleich.**

If you plan to see the person the next day, you can say:

Bis morgen.

Two very informal expressions that you frequently hear people use are:

Tschüs.　　　　　　　　**Tschau.**

Tschau is similar to the Italian expression *(ciao)* that is used in several European languages.

Aktivitäten

A　Go over to a classmate. Say "so long" to him or her and then return to your seat.

B　Work with a classmate. Say *tschüs* to one another and let each other know that you'll be getting together again soon.

C　Say "good-bye" to your teacher in German and then say "good-bye" to a friend. Don't forget to use a different expression with each person!

Mehr Sprechen

—Tag, Dieter.

　—Tag, Ingrid. Wie geht's?

—Gut, danke. Und dir?

　—Nicht schlecht, danke.

—Tschüs, Dieter.

　—Tschüs, Ingrid. Bis später.

Aktivitäten

A Work with a friend. Speak German together. Have fun saying as much as you can to one another!

B Look at these two photographs of German-speaking people saying "good-bye." Describe what the people are doing.

Kultur

Common First Names

The following are some common names used for boys and girls in German.

Jungen

Alexander, Bernd, Christoph, Dieter, Erich, Ernst, Fritz, Hans, Jochen, Jürgen, Klaus, Konrad, Martin, Max, Michael, Otto, Paul, Peter, Richard, Rudi, Stefan, Thomas, Willi

Mädchen

Anna, Beate, Brigitte, Christa, Christel, Dagmar, Elisabeth, Elke, Eva, Helga, Ingrid, Jutta, Luise, Margret, Monika, Paula, Petra, Rosa, Sabine, Susanne, Sylvia, Ursula

3 **Im Klassenzimmer**

Identifying Classroom Objects

To find out what something is, you ask:

Was ist das?

Das ist ____.

eine Tafel

ein Stuhl

ein Schreibtisch

ein Computer

ein Stück Papier

ein Buch

ein Tisch

ein Schwamm

eine Kreide

ein Heft

ein Rechner

ein Radiergummi

ein Block

ein Bleistift

ein Kugelschreiber

ein Rucksack

To ask for something in a polite way, you say:

Ein Stück Papier, bitte.

Aktivitäten

A Ask a classmate to identify the following items in German. Don't forget to ask politely! Your classmate will answer.

1.

2.

3.

4.

5.

6.

B Look at each picture and say in German what each person needs.

1. 2.

C Point to something in the classroom and ask a classmate what it is.

Kultur

Schools in Germany

In Germany there are three types of high school. When a student finishes elementary school, *die Grundschule,* he or she must decide what type of high school to attend. *Das Gymnasium* is for students who want an academic preparation. *Die Realschule* is for commercial or vocational preparation. *Die Hauptschule* is for general studies.

To complete studies in the *Gymnasium* and receive *das Abitur*—the *Gymnasium* diploma—you must study for nine years. *Das Abitur* is called *das Abi* in student jargon. The *Realschule* requires six years of study and the *Hauptschule* five years.

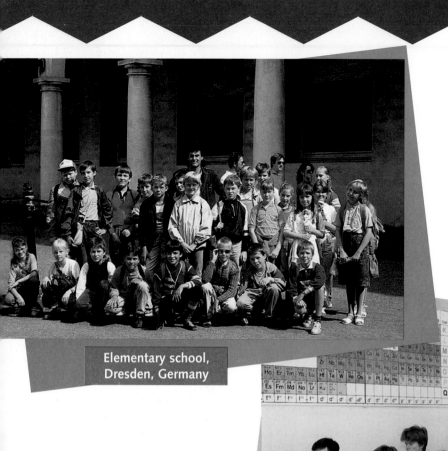

Elementary school,
Dresden, Germany

High school,
Munich, Germany

Vocational school,
Freiburg, Germany

4 ◆ **D**ie Zahlen

1	eins	16	sechzehn	30	dreißig
2	zwei	17	siebzehn	40	vierzig
3	drei	18	achtzehn	50	fünfzig
4	vier	19	neunzehn	60	sechzig
5	fünf	20	zwanzig	70	siebzig
6	sechs			80	achtzig
7	sieben	21	einundzwanzig	90	neunzig
8	acht	22	zweiundzwanzig		
9	neun	23	dreiundzwanzig	100	(ein) hundert
10	zehn	24	vierundzwanzig	200	zweihundert
		25	fünfundzwanzig	300	dreihundert
11	elf	26	sechsundzwanzig		
12	zwölf	27	siebenundzwanzig	1.000	(ein) tausend
13	dreizehn	28	achtundzwanzig	2.000	zweitausend
14	vierzehn	29	neunundzwanzig		
15	fünfzehn				

Kultur

Writing Numbers in German

In German-speaking countries, the numbers one and seven are written differently. Look at the photographs below to find these numbers. How are they written?

Aktivitäten

A Your teacher will write some numbers on the chalkboard. Then he or she will call out the number in German and ask a student to circle the correct number.

B Work with a classmate. One of you will count from 20 to 30. The other will count from 40 to 50.

C Have a contest with a friend in class. See who can count the fastest from 1 to 100 by tens!

D Work in groups of two. Take turns writing numbers on a piece of paper. Give the number your partner wrote on the paper.

Finding Out the Price

To find out how much something costs, you ask:

—Wieviel kostet der Rechner, Frau Schultz?

  —Vierzehn Euro.

—Danke schön.

Aktivität

A Work with a classmate.
One of you will be the customer
and the other will be the clerk
at a stationery store. Make up
a conversation to buy the
following things.

das Heft

der Rechner

14€

6€

der
Radiergummi

der Kugelschreiber

5€

1€

1€

der
Bleistift

25€

der
Rucksack

Kultur

Money Systems

The monetary unit of the Federal Republic of Germany and Austria is the *Euro.*

The Swiss monetary system is based on the Swiss franc, *Franken*. It is divided into 100 *Rappen*.

Aktivität

A Give the amount of each euro pictured below.

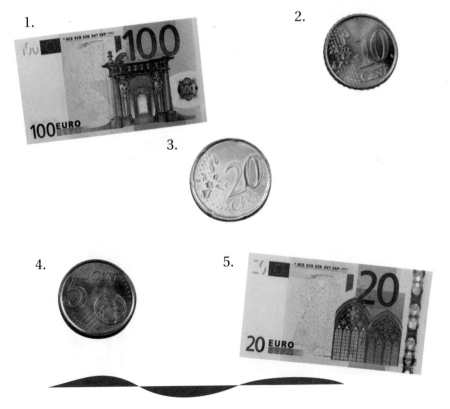

1.

2.

3.

4.

5.

Umgangsformen

Speaking Politely

—Guten Tag.
—Guten Tag. Eine Cola, bitte.

(*The waiter brings the order.*)
—Danke schön.
—Bitte sehr.

(*A little later.*)
—Wieviel kostet die Cola, bitte?
—Drei Euro.

No matter what language you speak, it is important to be polite. The following words mean "please," "thank you," and "you're welcome":

Bitte.

Danke sehr.   **Bitte sehr.**

Danke schön.   **Bitte schön.**

Aktivitäten

A With a friend, practice reading the dialogue on pages 246–247 aloud.

B You are at a café in a small German village along the Rhine. Order the following things. Ask a classmate to be the server.

1. eine Tasse Kaffee   2. eine Tasse Tee   3. eine Limonade

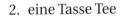

4. eine Cola   5. ein Mineralwasser

C You would like to order the following foods at a German restaurant. Be polite when you order them!

1. eine Bratwurst

2. eine Pizza

3. ein Stück Apfelstrudel

4. ein Wienerschnitzel

5. Sauerbraten

6. ein Omelett

Kultur

Foods of the German World

The cooking of Germany is extremely varied. Today many Germans are very health conscious. But when we think of typical German fare, we think of German sausage or *Wurst*. One of the most popular is *Bratwurst*. *Bratwurst* comes from Nürnberg and is made with seasoned, spiced pork. *Weisswurst* is made from veal and *Leberwurst* is made from liver.

Bauernwurst is a farmer's sausage, similar to *Knackwurst*. *Knackwurst* is very much like a *Frankfurter*, but a bit rounder. The *Frankfurter* comes from the city of Frankfurt, but it's probably more popular here in the US where it is called a "hot dog."

Small *Frankfurters* are called *Wiener*. In Germany, the word *Wiener* is more commonly used than *Frankfurter*. In Austria, however, the most popular word is *Frankfurter*.

Wurst, regardless of the type, is almost always eaten with a piece of bread and a dab of mustard.

Butcher shop,
Berlin, Germany

6 ◆ **D**ie Uhrzeit

To find out the time, you ask:

Wie spät ist es?

Wieviel Uhr ist es?

To tell the time, you say:

Es ist eins.
Es ist ein Uhr.

Es ist zwei
(Uhr).

Es ist drei
(Uhr).

Es ist vier
(Uhr).

Es ist fünf
(Uhr).

Es ist sechs
(Uhr).

Es ist sieben
(Uhr).

Es ist acht
(Uhr).

Es ist neun
(Uhr).

Es ist zehn
(Uhr).

Es ist elf
(Uhr).

Es ist zwölf
(Uhr).

Es ist ein Uhr fünf.   **Es ist zwei Uhr zehn.**   **Es ist fünf Uhr vierzig.**   **Es ist sechs Uhr fünfzehn.**   **Es ist halb acht.**
Es ist sieben Uhr dreißig.

Kultur

The 24-Hour Clock

In German, the 24-hour clock is used for schedules, radio and TV program guides, and for any official business.

Es ist vierzehn Uhr.

Es ist achtzehn Uhr.

In more informal situations, the 12-hour clock is used.

Es ist sieben Uhr.

Es ist elf Uhr.

When writing the time in numerals, German uses a period (.) rather than a colon (:).

9.00   9:00

19.00   19:00

Look at this German Christmas schedule of events. What do you notice about the times?

Programm

Christkindlesmarkt auf dem Hauptmarkt zu Nürnberg

28. November bis 24. Dezember

Freitag	28. Nov.	17.30	Eröffnungsfeier Opening Ceremony
Samstag	29. Nov.	17.00	
Sonntag	30. Nov.	15.00	
	und	17.00	
Montag	1. Dez.	19.00	
Dienstag	2. Dez.	19.00	Posaunenchor
Mittwoch	3. Dez.	18.00	Trombone concert
Donnerstag	4. Dez.	19.00	
Freitag	5. Dez.	19.00	
Samstag	6. Dez.	17.00	
Sonntag	7. Dez.	15.00	
	und	17.00	
Montag	8. Dez.	17.00	Kinderbescherung mit Kindersin-
Dienstag	9. Dez.	17.00	gen · Distribution of Christmas
Mittwoch	10. Dez.	17.00	presents among children with singing of carols
Donnerstag	11. Dez.	18.15	Lichterzug · Lantern procession
Freitag	12. Dez.	19.00	
Samstag	13. Dez.	17.00	
Sonntag	14. Dez.	15.00	
	und	17.00	
Montag	15. Dez.	19.00	
Dienstag	16. Dez.	19.00	
Mittwoch	17. Dez.	18.00	Posaunenchor ·
Donnerstag	18. Dez.	19.00	Trombone concert
Freitag	19. Dez.	19.00	
Samstag	20. Dez.	17.00	
Sonntag	21. Dez.	15.00	
	und	17.00	
Montag	22. Dez.	19.00	
Dienstag	23. Dez.	19.00	

Aktivität

A Give the time.

Telling At What Time

—Um wieviel Uhr findet das
 Konzert statt?

 —Das Konzert beginnt um
  neun Uhr.

Aktivität

A Work with a classmate. One of you will ask at what time
the following takes place. The other will answer.

1. das Konzert

2. der Film

3. die Party

4. das Theaterstück

7 Die Tage

Telling the Days of the Week

Sonnabend is also used for Saturday.

To find out and give the day, you say:

—Welcher Tag ist heute?
—Heute ist Montag.

—Und welcher Tag ist morgen?

—Morgen ist Dienstag.

Aktivität

A **Answer the following questions in German.**

1. Welcher Tag is heute?
2. Und welcher Tag ist morgen?

Kultur

Carnival

The celebration of Carnival is a happy time in most German-speaking areas. In Austria, Bavaria, and southern Germany, Carnival is called *der Fasching*. In Switzerland and the Black Forest area, it is called *die Fastnacht*. Along the Rhine River, it is called *der Karneval*.

Regardless of the word used, it is a time to make merry. People wear crazy costumes. They parade through the streets or they go to private parties or masked balls called *Maskenbälle*. The height of Carnival is the Sunday, Monday, and Tuesday before Ash Wednesday. Ash Wednesday is the first day of Lent, a time for fasting.

German Online

For more information about Carnival and other German celebrations, go to the Glencoe Web site: glencoe.com

Carnival, St. Gallen, Switzerland

German carnival masks

Garmisch Carnival, Bavaria, Germany

Die Monate und die Jahreszeiten

Telling the Months

JANUAR	FEBRUAR	MÄRZ	APRIL	MAI	JUNI
1 2 3 4 5 6	1 2 3	1 2	1 2 3 4 5 6	1 2 3 4	1
7 8 9 10 11 12 13	4 5 6 7 8 9 10	3 4 5 6 7 8 9	7 8 9 10 11 12 13	5 6 7 8 9 10 11	2 3 4 5 6 7 8
14 15 16 17 18 19 20	11 12 13 14 15 16 17	10 11 12 13 14 15 16	14 15 16 17 18 19 20	12 13 14 15 16 17 18	9 10 11 12 13 14 15
21 22 23 24 25 26 27	18 19 20 21 22 23 24	17 18 19 20 21 22 23	21 22 23 24 25 26 27	19 20 21 22 23 24 25	16 17 18 19 20 21 22
28 29 30 31	25 26 27 28 29	24 31 25 26 27 28 29 30	28 29 30	26 27 28 29 30 31	23 30 24 25 26 27 28 29

JULI	AUGUST	SEPTEMBER	OKTOBER	NOVEMBER	DEZEMBER
1 2 3 4 5 6	1 2 3	1 2 3 4 5 6 7	1 2 3 4 5	1 2	1 2 3 4 5 6 7
7 8 9 10 11 12 13	4 5 6 7 8 9 10	8 9 10 11 12 13 14	6 7 8 9 10 11 12	3 4 5 6 7 8 9	8 9 10 11 12 13 14
14 15 16 17 18 19 20	11 12 13 14 15 16 17	15 16 17 18 19 20 21	13 14 15 16 17 18 19	10 11 12 13 14 15 16	15 16 17 18 19 20 21
21 22 23 24 25 26 27	18 19 20 21 22 23 24	22 23 24 25 26 27 28	20 21 22 23 24 25 26	17 18 19 20 21 22 23	22 23 24 25 26 27 28
28 29 30 31	25 26 27 28 29 30 31	29 30	27 28 29 30 31	24 25 26 27 28 29 30	29 30 31

In Austria, January is called *Jänner.*

Telling the Seasons

der Frühling (im Frühling)

der Sommer (im Sommer)

der Herbst (im Herbst)

der Winter (im Winter)

Aktivitäten

A Make your own calendar in German. Label the months and the days of the week. Do it in the German style starting the week with Monday.

B Each of you will stand up in class and give in German the month in which you were born. Listen and keep a record of how many of you were born in the same month.

C Based on the information from *Aktivität B,* tell in German in which month most of the students in the class were born. Tell in which month the fewest were born.

D In which season of the year is . . . ?

1. Mai
2. Januar
3. August
4. Oktober

Frühling
Suppe

9 Das Wetter

—Wie ist das Wetter?
  —Das Wetter ist schön.
    Es ist schön.
    Es ist sonnig.

—Das Wetter ist nicht schön.
  Es ist schlecht.
  Es ist bewölkt.
  Es regnet.

Es ist windig.

Es schneit.

Es ist nicht warm. Es ist heiß.

Es ist nicht kühl. Es ist kalt.

Aktivitäten

A Tell in German what the weather is like today.

B Work in groups of four. Write in German the name of each season on a separate sheet of paper. Put the papers in a pile. Each of you will pull one sheet from the pile. Then describe the weather of the season written on the sheet.

C Draw a picture of your favorite type of weather. Then describe your picture to the class in German.

Kultur

Vacation Spots

In the south of Germany, there are some popular winter ski resorts. Garmisch-Partenkirchen is not far from Munich. There are also many ski resorts in the German-speaking section of Switzerland and in Austria.

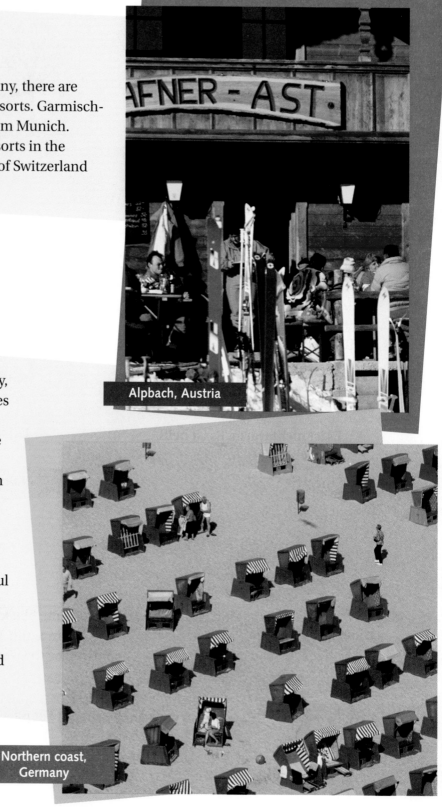

Alpbach, Austria

In the north of Germany, there are some lovely beaches that are popular in the summer. Since these beaches are on the North Sea, the water stays chilly and there is often a breeze. For this reason, people frequently sit in a *Strandkorb* to protect themselves from the wind.

There are some beautiful islands in the North Sea—Amrum, Sylt, and Spikeroog among them. Sylt, a popular vacation center, is connected to the mainland by a dam.

Northern coast, Germany

10

Ich heiße... und ich komme aus...

—Wie heißt du?

   —Ich heiße Katerina Weiss. Und wie heißt du?

—Ich heiße Werner Hoffmann.

   —Woher kommst du, Werner?

—Ich komme aus Hannover. Und du, Katerina, woher kommst du?

   —Ich komme aus Houston.

—Ach so, du kommst aus den USA.

When you hear a question with –st in German: *heißt du?*, *kommst du?*, you answer with -e: *ich heiße, ich komme. Du* is used to speak to a friend and *ich* is used to speak about yourself.

heißt du?   **ich heiße**

kommst du?   **ich komme**

Aktivitäten

A **Walk around the classroom. Greet each of your classmates. Find out who each one is. Let each one know who you are.**

B **Get a beach ball. One person throws the ball as he or she asks, *Woher kommst du?* The one who catches the ball answers, *Ich komme aus...***

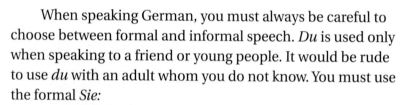

When speaking German, you must always be careful to choose between formal and informal speech. *Du* is used only when speaking to a friend or young people. It would be rude to use *du* with an adult whom you do not know. You must use the formal *Sie:*

Wie heißen Sie?

Woher kommen Sie, Herr Braun?

Aktivität

A Draw and cut out five stick figures. Give each one a name. Some will be stick figures of your friends and others will be of your teacher. Greet each of your stick figures in German. Ask their names and where they're from. Remember to use different terms with your friends and teachers!

Kultur

The German-Speaking World

Here are two friends from different areas of Europe. They both have something very important in common. They both speak German.

> Wie geht's? Ich heiße
> Peter und ich komme
> aus Reutte in Österreich.
> Ich spreche Deutsch.

> Wie geht's? Ich heiße
> Ingrid. Ich komme
> aus Gstaad in der Schweiz.
> Ich spreche auch Deutsch.

Welcome to
Japanese!

Mt. Fuji, Japan

Japanese is a fascinating language that is very different from many of the world's other languages. Japanese, unlike Spanish or German, does not belong to one of the major language families.

Japanese is the official language of Japan, a country of four main islands and 1042 smaller islands in the western Pacific. It is spoken by approximately 120 million people.

The Japanese make a great effort to be polite. They are almost apologetic in their speech. They do not want to offend. This desire has a great impact on the language. There are many polite and honorific forms in the Japanese language. A young person speaking to a friend will express the same idea in a different way when speaking to an older person. A woman would also express herself in a different way from a man.

For the Japanese, the group is more important than the individual. Japanese people always take into account the family or the company they work for before thinking of themselves.

Japan is a highly developed and industrialized country. It is a major economic and political force in the world today. A knowledge of its language and culture is a very valuable tool.

"Great Buddha," Kanakura, Japan

Tokyo, Japan

Rural village, Japan

Japanese to English

There are some Japanese words used in English. Do you know any of these words?

obi

ryokan

sushi

tatami

tempura

tsunami

1 Jiko shookai

Making Introductions

—Sumimasen. Hanada-san desu ka[?]
   —Hai, soo desu.
—Buraun desu. Hajimemashite. Doozo yoroshiku.
   —Hanada desu. Hajimemashite. Doozo yoroshiku.

Desu is similar to the verb "to be." Unlike English and the other languages you may have studied, *desu* is used for all forms: "am, is, are."

To form a question in Japanese, you put *ka* at the end of a statement. *Ka* is called a particle and it is like a question mark.

Statement: **Buraun desu.**

Question: **Hanada-san desu ka[?]**

Differences in Meaning

Japanese are extremely polite when they speak to each other. This is one of the reasons why the literal meaning of many Japanese expressions is often different from the informal meaning in English. For example, *Hajimemashite* is used to express "How do you do?" Literally, it means "It's the first time we meet." *Doozo yoroshiku* can express "It's nice to meet you" but it means "Please regard me favorably."

Sumimasen is an expression of apology, similar to "excuse me" or "I'm sorry." It is used to get someone's attention.

Names and Titles

When Japanese people introduce themselves, they often give their family name, not their first name. They give their family name with no title:

Hanada   **Okura**   **Yamaguchi**

When addressing others, however, they use the person's family name and a respectful title. There are many different honorific titles, but one of the most common is *san*. *San* is the equivalent of "Mr." or "Ms." in English. It is used for both males and females. Japanese never use *san* when talking about themselves.

Hanada-san   **Okura-san**   **Yamaguchi-san**

Activities

A   **Let's practice saying all of the Japanese expressions we know.**

—Sumimasen.

  —Hajimemashite.

—Doozo yoroshiku.

  —Hanada-san desu ka[?]

—Hai, soo desu.

  —Buraun desu.

B   Work with a classmate and ask each other your names.

—Sumimasen. _____-san desu ka[?]

  —Hai, soo desu.

—_____ desu.

C   You are visiting Roppongi, a popular section of Tokyo. Reply to a Japanese person who says the following to you.

1. (Your name)-san desu ka[?]
2. Hajimemashite.
3. Doozo yoroshiku.

Roppongi District,
Tokyo, Japan

D   Here's a photograph of Japanese teenagers who live in Kyoto. Describe their clothing. Is it like yours?

E Work with a classmate and have the following conversation in Japanese. Excuse yourselves. Ask one another "How do you do?" and introduce yourselves. Say that you are happy to meet.

Culture

Fashion in Japan

Modern Tokyo is probably one of the most fashionable cities in the world. The Japanese are very fashion-conscious. Look at these photographs of department store windows and people on the streets of Tokyo.

Shibuya District, Tokyo, Japan

Ginza, Tokyo, Japan

There is also a traditional Japanese dress—the *kimono*. Today it is worn only on formal occasions such as weddings.

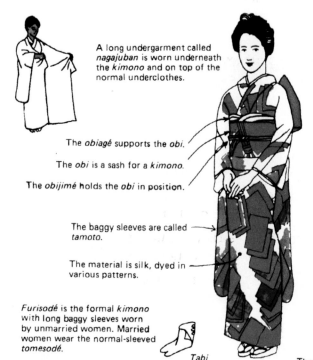

A long undergarment called *nagajuban* is worn underneath the *kimono* and on top of the normal underclothes.

The *obiagé* supports the *obi*.

The *obi* is a sash for a *kimono*.

The *obijimé* holds the *obi* in position.

The baggy sleeves are called *tamoto*.

The material is silk, dyed in various patterns.

Furisodé is the formal *kimono* with long baggy sleeves worn by unmarried women. Married women wear the normal-sleeved *tomesodé*.

Tabi

Japanese Online

For more information about Japanese traditions, go to the Glencoe Web site: glencoe.com

The *montsuki* or *haori*: a half-coat emblazoned with the wearer's family crest.

Mon: crest

Sensu: folding fan

Hakama: a culotte-like garment worn over the *kimono*

Tabi should be worn with *montsuki*.

Formal wear

The *obi* is made either of stiff material (the *kaku-obi*) or of soft material (the *heko-obi*).

Less formal wear

2 ◆ *Go-aisatsu*

Greeting People

—Konnichi wa.
  —Konnichi wa. O-genki
  desu ka[?]
—Hai, arigatoo gozaimasu.
  Yamaguchi-san wa[?]
  —Genki desu.

Kobe, Japan

The following are Japanese greetings to be said at various times of the day:

Ohayoo gozaimasu.
(morning)

Konnichi wa. *(day)*

Konban wa. *(evening)*

Culture

Formality and Politeness

When speaking Japanese, you must always consider the level of formality in your speech. The question, *O-genki desu ka[?]* literally means "How have you been lately?" so you do not say it to anyone you've seen recently. You use it only when you haven't seen a person in a while and you want to know about his or her health. There can be several answers to the question *O-genki desu ka[?]* From formal to informal, they are:

1. **Ee, genki desu.**
2. **Okagesama de, genki desu.**
3. **Ee okagesama de.**
4. **Hai, arigatoo gozaimasu.**

The expression "How are you?" in English is a way of saying "hello" rather than a question about your health. In Japan, a comment about the weather serves the same purpose. Someone may greet you and say:

Ii o-tenki desu ne[?] The weather's quite nice, no?

In response, you don't have to give an opinion or comment, just be polite and agree:

Soo desu ne.

Greeting Someone You've Seen Recently

—Okura-san, ohayoo gozaimasu.

—Aa, Kawamura-san, ohayoo.

—Ii o-tenki desu ne[?]

—Ee, soo desu ne.

The particle *ne* at the end of the sentence can serve many purposes. With a high intonation, *ne* is used to ask for someone's agreement:

Ii o-tenki desu ne[?]　　　　Don't you think? That's right, isn't it?

When said with a falling intonation and extended to *nee,* the particle indicates that you agree with what the speaker is saying:

Soo desu nee.

Activities

A　**Let's practice saying the Japanese expressions we know.**

—Ohayoo gozaimasu.

　Konnichi wa.

　Konban wa.

—O-genki desu ka[?]

　Ee, genki desu.

　Okagesama de, genki desu.

　Ee okagesama de.

　Hai, arigatoo gozaimasu.

—Ii o-tenki desu ne[?]

　Soo desu ne.

B　**You are visiting Yokohama, located just outside of Tokyo. Speak to the person in Japanese who says the following to you.**

1. Konnichi wa.

2. Ohayoo gozaimasu.

3. O-genki desu ka[?]

4. Ii o-tenki desu ne[?]

Yokohama, Japan

C Get up from your desk and walk around the room. Greet several of your classmates in Japanese.

D Work with a classmate. Make up the following conversation in Japanese. Greet one another. You haven't seen each other in a while. You're both interested in knowing how the other is doing.

Culture

Ojigi

The traditional Japanese greeting is not a handshake but a bow from the waist. A bow is called *ojigi,* and is a way of showing both respect and affection.

This greeting can vary from a slight bow to a very low bow. It depends upon the relationship of the people and the amount of respect they wish to show.

Businessmen, Osaka, Japan

Department store greeter, Tokyo, Japan

3 ◆ *Wakareru toki ni...*

Saying "Good-bye"

—Hayashi-san, shitsurei shimasu.
Sayoonara.

Dewa, mata.

Ja, mata.

Shitsurei shimasu is a formal way to say "good-bye." It literally means "excuse me."

Sayoonara, the beautiful Japanese expression we hear used in English, is used to express a farewell to a person whom you do not plan to see again soon.

To say "see you later," you would use *dewa, mata* if you wish to be very formal. Less formal is *ja, mata.*

Activities

A Walk around the room. Say "good-bye" to some of your class-mates in a formal way.

B Walk around the room and say "good-bye" to some of your classmates in a very informal way.

Reviewing All We Know

—Hanada-san, ohayoo gozaimasu.

　—Aa, Buraun-san, ohayoo.

—Ii o-tenki desu ne[?]

　—Ee, soo desu ne.

—Shitsurei shimasu.

　—Ja, mata.

Activities

A   You are in the large city of Osaka. Reply to the following.

1. _____-san desu ka[?]
2. Konnichi wa.
3. Ii o-tenki desu ne[?]

4. O-genki desu ka[?]
5. Dewa, mata.

B   Work with a friend. Speak Japanese together. Have fun saying as much as you can to each other.

Osaka, Japan

Culture

Written Japanese

Modern Japanese is written using three different writing systems. They are called *hiragana, katakana,* and *kanji.*

Hiragana and *katakana* have symbols that represent sounds much like the Roman alphabet. The *kanji* are Chinese characters. They are ideographs that represent sound and meaning. The *kanji* were taken to Japan in the fifth century. Before this time, Japan had no writing system. Since the *kanji* were designed for a completely different language, *hiragana* and *katakana* symbols were created. Each letter of *hiragana* and *katakana* represents one syllable. Each of these alphabets has 48 symbols. All sounds of the Japanese language can be represented in print using these two alphabets.

Katakana is used for foreign words used in Japanese other than Chinese or Korean. For example, *hottodoggu* and *hanbaagaa* are written in *katakana*.

Here is a Japanese food ad. Note the examples of the three writing systems.

katakana = "house"

kanji = "foodstuffs"

hiragana

katakana

Identifying Classroom Objects

To find out what something is, you ask:

—**Nan desu ka[?]**

isu

kami

hon

tsukue

konpyuutaa

kokuban-keshi

chooku

nooto

keisanki

keshigomu

paddo

booru-pen

enpitsu

kaban

Japanese nouns do not have different forms for the singular and plural. For example, the word *hon* means both "book" and "books."

Activities

A   Point to something in the classroom that you know how to say in Japanese. Ask a classmate what it is and have him or her respond.

B   Look at each picture and say in Japanese what each person needs.

1.

2.

3.

4.

*C*ulture

Schools in Japan

Schools in Japan are very strict and students must work very hard. They take competitive exams even to enter some elementary schools!

Japanese students attend six years of elementary school, three years of junior high school, and three years of high school. They start school at age seven. Uniforms are not worn in elementary school. Recently, however, yellow hats or helmets are often required for traffic safety.

Most junior high school students wear a uniform. It is still common to see boys of this age wearing a black, military-looking uniform called a *tsume-eri*. Girls wear a black or navy blue sailor suit called a *seeraa-fuku*.

Senior high students must study a great deal to prepare themselves for many difficult university entrance exams.

5 Suu-ji

Numbers

	0	rei, zero				
一	1	ichi	11	juu-ichi	21	ni-juu-ichi
二	2	ni	12	juu-ni	28	ni-juu-hachi
三	3	san	13	juu-san	30	san-juu
四	4	shi, yon	14	juu-shi, juu-yon	40	yon-juu
五	5	go	15	juu-go	50	go-juu
六	6	roku	16	juu-roku	60	roku-juu
七	7	shichi, nana	17	juu-shichi, juu-nana	70	nana-juu
八	8	hachi	18	juu-hachi	80	hachi-juu
九	9	ku, kyuu	19	juu-ku, juu-kyuu	90	kyu-juu
十	10	juu	20	ni-juu	100	hyaku

Activities

A Your teacher will write some numbers on the chalkboard. Then he or she will call out the number in Japanese and ask a student to circle the correct number.

B Count from 1 to 10 aloud.

C Work with a classmate. One of you will count from 20 to 30. The other will count from 40 to 50.

D Have a contest with a friend. See who can count the fastest from 1 to 100 by tens.

E Work in groups of two. Take turns writing numbers from 1 to 100 on a piece of paper. Give the number your partner wrote on the paper in Japanese.

Culture

Japanese Currency

The monetary unit in Japan is the *yen,* often pronounced "en." Presently, there are coins for 1, 5, 10, 50, 100, and 500 yen. There are also bills for 1,000; 5,000; and 10,000 yen.

6 ◆ *Jikan*

Telling Time

To find out the time, you ask:

—**Sumimasen. Nan-ji desu ka[?]**

To answer, you say:

—**Ni-ji han desu. (2:30)**

ichi-ji

ni-ji

san-ji

yo-ji

go-ji

roku-ji

shichi-ji

hachi-ji

ku-ji

juu-ji

juu-ichi-ji

juu-ni-ji

shichi-ji-han

Activity

A Give the times on the clocks below.

7 Resutoran de...

At a Restaurant

—Sumimasen. Piza wa arimasu ka[?]

—Hai, arimasu.

—Jaa. Piza o kudasai.

Ordering Food

If you want to ask if someone has something, you ask *arimasu* with the question particle *ka*.

If the answer is yes, you would say *hai*.

arimasu ka[?]   **hai, arimasu**

Pronounce the following Japanese words for different foods. You should have little trouble guessing what they mean:

sarada	**suupu**
piza	**supagetti**
juusu	

When you order these foods, you would use the particle *o* followed by *kudasai* to be polite. *Kudasai* is similar to the English "please."

Piza o kudasai.

As you can see from this Japanese ad, pizza is popular in Japan.

Activity

A **You are at a restaurant in Tokyo. Order the following foods. Ask a classmate to be your server. Then switch parts.**

1. piza
2. hanbaagaa
3. chiizu baagaa
4. chikin baagaa
5. supagetti

6. suupu
7. juusu
8. bifuteki
9. omuretsu
10. sarada

Ginza, Tokyo, Japan

Finding Out How Much Something Costs

—Sumimasen. Hanbaagaa wa arimasu ka[?]

—Hai, arimasu.

—Ikura desu ka[?]

—Ni-hyaku-ni-juu (220)-en desu.

—Jaa, hanbaagaa to furaido poteto o onegai-shimasu.

—Arigatoo gozaimasu. Yon-hyaku (400)-en desu.

Note that a polite way to ask a server for something is:

... o onegai-shimasu.

To find out how much something costs, you ask:

—**Ikura desu ka[?]**

—**Ni-hyaku (200)-en desu.**

The particle *to* means "and":

hanbaagaa *to* onion ringu

Activities

A   Read the conversation on page 289 with a classmate. Remember to use as much expression as possible!

B   Order the following foods. Ask a classmate to be your server. Then switch parts. Don't forget to be polite and say *o onegai-shimasu*.

1. omuretsu
2. supagetti
3. fisshu baagaa
4. onion ringu
5. chikin suupu

Culture

Japanese Food

Although Japanese food is quite different from American-style food, Japanese restaurants are becoming popular here in the United States, especially in big cities. You may even know what the following dishes are:

Nihon ryoori

sushi

sashimi

tempura

sukiyaki

teriyaki

udon

soba

shabu shabu

Here is a typical take-out menu for a sushi restaurant.

In Japanese restaurants you'll usually be given a pair of half-split wooden chopsticks, called *wari-bashi,* in a paper envelope. In Japanese homes, however, re-usable sticks of various materials are used.

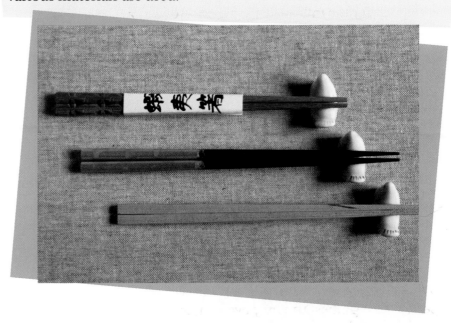

In restaurant windows there are true-to-life wax or plastic models of the dishes to be ordered. These are called *sampuru.*

8 Nani-go o hanashimasu ka[?]

Telling What I Speak

—Sumimasen. Nihongo o hanashimasu ka[?]

—Hai, (nihongo o) hanashimasu.

—Eigo o hanashimasu ka[?]

—Hai, (eigo o) hanashimasu.

When you hear the question *hanashimasu ka[?]*, you answer *hanashimasu* if the the answer is "yes":

hanashimasu ka[?]   **hai, hanashimasu**

If the answer is "no", you answer with *hanashimasen*:

hanashimasu ka[?]   **iie, hanashimasen**

—Sumimasen. Nihongo o hanashimasu ka[?]

—Iie, hanashimasen.

(or)

Hai, sukoshi hanashimasu.

Let's do the same with "to understand."

wakarimasu ka[?]   **hai, wakarimasu**

wakarimasu ka[?]   **iie, wakarimasen**

—Sumimasen. Nihongo ga wakarimasu ka[?]

  —Iie, wakarimasen.

   (or)

   Hai, sukoshi wakarimasu.

Activities

Konnichi wa und moin moin!

Für einen modernen Wirtschaftsstandort wie Schleswig-Holstein ist ein vielseitiges Kultur- und Freizeitangebot genauso wichtig wie der aufgeschlossene Umgang miteinander. Ob Arbeitnehmer oder Unternehmer, ob in Husum, Kiel oder Tokio geboren – die Menschen leben und arbeiten hier einfach gern. Internationalität und Gastfreundschaft werden bei uns großgeschrieben – so groß, daß in Halstenbek eine japanische Schule errichtet wurde. Das zeigt, daß uns auch die „fernsten" Interessen ganz nah am Herzen liegen.

Schleswig-Holstein ■
Die Luft, die Zukunft atmet ■

Do you recognize the two languages in this ad?

A **Answer the following questions in Japanese with "yes."**

1. Nihongo o hanashimasu ka[?]
2. Eigo o hanashimasu ka[?]
3. Nihongo no hon ga arimasu ka[?]
4. Booru-pen ga arimasu ka[?]
5. Nihongo ga wakarimasu ka[?]
6. Eigo ga wakarimasu ka[?]

B **Answer the following questions in Japanese with "no."**

1. Nihongo o hanashimasu ka[?]
2. Nihongo no hon ga arimasu ka[?]
3. Nihongo ga wakarimasu ka[?]

9 **N**an-nichi, nan-yoobi

Telling the Days of the Week

nichiyoobi

kayoobi

mokuyoobi

doyoobi

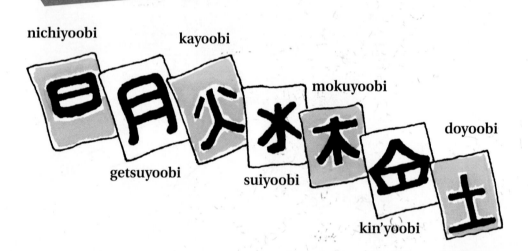

getsuyoobi

suiyoobi

kin'yoobi

To find out and give the day of the week, you say:

–Nan'yoobi desu ka[?]

  –Getsuyoobi desu.

Telling the Months

ICHI-GATSU	NI-GATSU	SAN-GATSU	SHI-GATSU	GO-GATSU	ROKO-GATSU
1 2 3 4 5 6 7 8 9 10 11 12 13 14 15 16 17 18 19 20 21 22 23 24 25 26 27 28 29 30 31	1 2 3 4 5 6 7 8 9 10 11 12 13 14 15 16 17 18 19 20 21 22 23 24 25 26 27 28 29	1 2 3 4 5 6 7 8 9 10 11 12 13 14 15 16 17 18 19 20 21 22 23 24 25 26 27 28 29 30 31	1 2 3 4 5 6 7 8 9 10 11 12 13 14 15 16 17 18 19 20 21 22 23 24 25 26 27 28 29 30	1 2 3 4 5 6 7 8 9 10 11 12 13 14 15 16 17 18 19 20 21 22 23 24 25 26 27 28 29 30 31	1 2 3 4 5 6 7 8 9 10 11 12 13 14 15 16 17 18 19 20 21 22 23 24 25 26 27 28 29 30

SHICHI-GATSU	HACHI-GATSU	KU-GATSU	JUU-GATSU	JUU-ICHI-GATSU	JUU-NI-GATSU
1 2 3 4 5 6 7 8 9 10 11 12 13 14 15 16 17 18 19 20 21 22 23 24 25 26 27 28 29 30 31	1 2 3 4 5 6 7 8 9 10 11 12 13 14 15 16 17 18 19 20 21 22 23 24 25 26 27 28 29 30 31	1 2 3 4 5 6 7 8 9 10 11 12 13 14 15 16 17 18 19 20 21 22 23 24 25 26 27 28 29 30	1 2 3 4 5 6 7 8 9 10 11 12 13 14 15 16 17 18 19 20 21 22 23 24 25 26 27 28 29 30 31	1 2 3 4 5 6 7 8 9 10 11 12 13 14 15 16 17 18 19 20 21 22 23 24 25 26 27 28 29 30	1 2 3 4 5 6 7 8 9 10 11 12 13 14 15 16 17 18 19 20 21 22 23 24 25 26 27 28 29 30 31

To find out a person's birthday month, you ask:

—Yamaguchi-san no o-tanjoobi wa nan-gatsu desu ka[?]

—Tanjoobi wa roku-gatsu desu.

Activities

A   Give the days of the week you go to school in Japanese. Then give the days of the week you don't go to school.

B   Answer the following questions.

1. Nan'yoobi desu ka[?]
2. O-tanjoobi wa nan-gatsu desu ka[?]

C   Each of you will stand up and give your birthday month in Japanese. Listen and keep a record of how many of you were born in the same month.

Japanese festivals

D   Based on the information from *Activity C,* tell in Japanese in which month most of the students in the class were born. Tell in which month the fewest were born.